Alone
with
God

Alone with God

Campbell McAlpine

BETHANY HOUSE PUBLISHERS

MINNEAPOLIS, MINNESOTA 55438

A Division of Bethany Fellowship, Inc.

Published in England by Marshall Morgan and Scott under the title,
The Practice of Biblical Meditation

Copyright © 1981
Campbell McAlpine
ISBN 0-87123-000-3

Published by Bethany Fellowship, Inc.
6820 Auto Club Road, Minneapolis, Minnesota 55438

Printed in the United States of America

My God, I thank Thee for Thy Word
That comes like medicine or a sword,
To change my life that I may be,
In greater likeness unto Thee.
Speak how Thou wilt, that is Thy choice,
In thunders peal or still small voice,
Thy Word is truth, Thy Word is light
To show me how to live aright.

Reveal Thyself that is my plea
Reveal Thyself O God to me,
Show me Thy will, show me Thy ways,
That I may serve Thee all my days.

'Let there be light' you once did cry,
And brilliant radiance filled the sky,
Command again that light to me,
That I may more Thy glory see.

Thou Living Word, I praise Thy Name
Thou art forevermore the same,
You spoke to prophet, priest and king
Then speak to me, Thy word do bring.

I thirst for Thee My God, My Lord
And Open up Thy sacred Word,
I come to drink, I come to feed,
Then meet my very deepest need.

Come Holy Ghost, come heavenly dove,
Show me my Lord, the One I love
And speak to me that I may say,
Yes . . . God spoke to me today.

Give me Lord Thy revelation
Through Thy Word in meditation,
And let it ever to me bring,
The knowledge of my Lord and King.

Campbell McAlpine

Contents

Preface

This manual has been written without any claim to literary expertise, or a desire to be known as an 'author', but because of a very clear direction by God to put in writing some of the principles of biblical meditation.

The rewards of this devotional approach to the Word of God are such that no earthly wealth could purchase them, because the knowledge of God and his beloved Son, Jesus, to quote the psalmist David, 'is better unto me than thousands of gold and silver'. The greatest need in the lives of those who claim to have a relationship with God, through the Lord Jesus Christ, is an ever increasing knowledge of God himself.

We have moved into the time the prophet Isaiah predicted: 'For, behold, the darkness shall cover the earth, and gross darkness the people: *But* the Lord shall arise upon thee, and his glory shall be seen upon thee' (Isa. 60:2). The Church of the living God has to stand, and stand upright, that the power of the Almighty might be manifested through her.

Daniel, the prophet, reminded us however, that 'the people that do know their God shall be strong, and do exploits, and they that have understanding among the people shall instruct many' (Dan. 11:32–3). The purpose of meditation is to give us, not only knowledge, but understanding.

The most important words written in this book are scriptures. I encourage the reader to carefully and prayerfully read each one, because it is through God's Word that light comes.

Acknowledgement and loving gratitude to my wife, Shelagh, our family and friends, for their constant source of encouragement. A very special thank you to Stuart, our son, whose help and advice was invaluable.

For all who contributed time to the preparation, typing and copying of this manuscript, I express my deepest appreciation.

Introduction

Welcome, as a reader of this book. Without any exaggeration, if you read it and apply its truths, it will revolutionise your life. This is not a man originated assertion, but a God given promise to those who will meditate day and night in the Word of God:

He shall be like a tree planted by the rivers of water, that bringeth forth his fruit in his season; his leaf also shall not wither; and whatsoever he doeth shall prosper (Ps. 1:3).

The book is written in two parts. The first part is called PRE-MEDITATION. The dictionary meaning of this word is 'to deliberate beforehand'. This we will do, and consider certain subjects which are essentially linked with meditating in the Word of God. The second part is under the heading of MEDITATION, where we consider the meaning and practice of this devotional exercise.

Note: the use of italics for emphasis in quoting Scripture is the author's own.

Part 1
PRE-MEDITATION

... sound an alarm in my holy mountain: let all the inhabitants of the land tremble: for the day of the Lord cometh, for it is nigh at hand (Joel 2:1).

For the Lord himself shall descend from heaven with a shout, with the voice of the archangel, and with the trump of God: and the dead in Christ shall rise first:

Then we which are alive and remain shall be caught up together with them in the clouds, to meet the Lord in the air: and so shall we ever be with the Lord (1 Thess. 4:16–17).

1 *Meditation* . . .

its need

How can we attract a person's attention? A baby turns in its cot in the night and immediately a mother is fully alert, yet a thunder storm can fail to awaken a deep sleeper. I once heard of a preacher who could not sleep in a room if there was a clock ticking, yet he slept through a noisy car collision that occurred a few yards from his bedroom window. Different sounds attract our attention in a variety of ways and to varying degrees, but beyond all these, the God of heaven and earth is trying to gain our attention in these days, because there are vital concerns he wishes to share, and messages he wants the world to hear, the Church to hear, you to hear.

In the middle of the last century, a noted French scientist, Pierre Berchelt, stated his belief that within one hundred years scientists would have discovered the secret of the atom. He went on to suggest that such a breakthrough would herald the age in which God would say to the world, 'Gentlemen, it is closing time!' Cartoonists sometimes humorously depict placard carriers with such messages as 'The end is near' or 'Prepare to meet thy God', but the time is fast approaching when such humour will be reality. A trumpet will sound, and the Lord Christ will descend from heaven. The 'last days' will have run their course, prophecy will have been fulfilled, and as James Black wrote in his hymn, 'When the roll is called up yonder . . . time shall be no more.' However, in his grace, God provides shrill, clear and sometimes piercing bugle blasts to draw our attention to neglected truths to equip us for these present momentous days; to instruct us in the way we should go; to warn us of dangers and diversions, so that we might do the will of God

3

on earth as it is done in heaven, and one day be presented faultless before the presence of his glory with exceeding joy. It is hoped that this manual will serve as such a bugle, to inspire you to know God better, to delight in Him, to encourage you to continue in the things which you have already learned, to exhort you to 'be perfect, thoroughly furnished unto all good works', and to prepare you to be effective in the kingdom of God.

Effectiveness is dependent on our knowledge of God, and this is the main purpose of biblical meditation – that we might know him. It was revealed to Daniel that at the time of the end 'many shall run to and fro, and knowledge shall be increased' (Dan. 12:4), but with all the increase of knowledge in so many different fields, bringing with it an increased vocabulary, the greatest knowledge of all is still the knowledge of God. To emphasise this truth Jeremiah recorded, 'Thus saith the Lord, let not the wise man glory in his wisdom, neither let the mighty man glory in his might, let not the rich man glory in his riches: But let him that glorieth glory in this, that he understandeth and knoweth me, that I am the Lord which exercise lovingkindness, judgment, and righteousness, in the earth: for in these things I delight, saith the Lord' (Jer. 9:23–4). Thank God, he is a God who can be known, and through the means of the Word of God this knowledge can be increased day by day.

Wherever there is the real, there is the counterfeit. One of the deceits that has ensnared millions is that true peace and tranquility can be obtained through transcendental meditation. However, the 'mantra' cannot replace the revelation by the Holy Spirit. Transcendental meditation seeks to provide a counterfeit practice for men and women who have been created to meditate on God, his character, his words, his works and his ways. Claiming to be non-religious, yet part Eastern and part humanistic in its philosophy, it declares that the answer to man's questions, and object of his quest, is within him, and that it is possible for the meditator to arrive at a mental state free from thought, imagery and symbol; a state called 'pure being', or 'bliss consciousness', the source of all thought. It fails to acknowledge or deal with man's greatest problem – his sin – and therefore eliminates the need of God's answer – a Saviour – Jesus Christ the Lord. It is not within the scope of this manual to give an account of the techniques of transcendental meditation, but to positively assert the teaching of the Word of God about biblical meditation, and to encourage the reader to become established in its practice.

A friend of ours, Tryna, who had been involved in transcendental meditation before she came to know the Lord Jesus in a personal way, had this to say:

> We used to descend down into ourselves, firmly and consistently pushing away all distracting thoughts. Our goal was to arrive at a state of nothingness, which we called peace. I would settle down into a void of blackness, a darkness which could be felt.
>
> What a difference biblical meditation has brought to my life. Here God's Word is the focus instead of self; satisfaction instead of emptiness; insight instead of darkness. Here was revelation from God instead of another mystical experience. I found power in God's Word to heal me and cleanse my mind, feed and satisfy my soul, and strengthen my spirit. Revelation 3:20 became especially meaningful: 'If any man hear my voice and open the door, I will come in to him, and sup with him and he with me.' I learned to hear God's voice.

We trust that you will hear the bugle call above all the sounds and voices which clamour for attention. The clamour of voices, with their conflicting solutions, resurrect the image of Babel as we realise the full weight and force of the linguistic inquisition that assaults our minds, but thank God 'there is a place of quiet rest' where the voice of the Creator of the universe can be heard, when we can say in humility, but certainty, 'God spoke to me today.'

This is being written at the beginning of the eighties. Already this decade is being called 'the decade of destiny'. We slip into a new decade with international problems, the possibility of shortages in energy and other commodities, the rattle of sabres, rising inflation, starving millions, and total evidence of conditions which the Bible said would prevail in the last time. The apostle Paul, referring to these times, wrote about the 'mystery of iniquity', warning that minds would be stormed and thoughts captured by 'all deceivableness of unrighteousness'. He warned about seducing spirits and doctrines of devils, and commands young Timothy to give himself to reading, exhortation and doctrine. 'Meditate on these things; give thyself wholly to them; that thy profiting may appear to all' (1 Tim. 4:15). God spoke through the prophet Isaiah and through him sounded the bugle call: 'Arise, shine; for thy light is come, and the glory of the Lord is risen upon thee. For behold darkness shall cover the earth, and gross darkness the people; but the Lord shall arise upon thee and his glory shall be seen upon thee' (Isa. 60:1–2).

It is true that the darkness is getting darker, but on many occasions God moved when things were at their worst. It was when the earth 'was without form and void, and darkness was upon the face of the waters' that God said, 'let there be light, and there was light'. It was when the children of Israel were in the gross darkness of their slavery in Egypt that God said, 'I am come down to deliver them.' It was when Palestine was under the Roman heel and religion had become a formality that the 'dayspring from on high' visited us. God's answer to darkness is his own glorious light. The more we inwardly receive truth, the more light there is within us. The more light in us, the more in the Church. The more light in the Church, the more light in the world. The meditator in the Word of God will be a recipient of truth and light, and therefore prepared to be a declarer of truth and a light that shines in a dark place.

The following is presented in manual form because it is our hope that this publication will be used as a practical learning aid, thus emphasising the need for the reader to be an efficient and studious learner. When a truth is important and life changing, it deserves our full concentration.

To merely read a book, be interested in its contents, or challenged by its message, is not necessarily to learn. It is our prayer that by the time you have read this manual you will be a meditator in the Word of God, applying the principles taught, increasing your knowledge of God and your capacity and ability to give him pleasure, and ready to teach someone else.

Biblical meditation will revolutionise your life when it becomes a continual part of your devotion and a consistent feature of your life. As the words of men swirl around you, you will discover that your meditation transforms your own communication, and you will join again with the Psalmist in his request, 'Let the words of my mouth and the meditation of my heart be acceptable in thy sight, O Lord, my strength and my redeemer' (Ps. 19:14).

The Lord bless you as you read.

APPLICATION

How very gracious of God to make his wisdom available to us, so that we can understand and know him. Why not appropriate the promise he gives through James

If any of you lack wisdom, let him ask of God who giveth to all men liberally, and upbraideth not, and it shall be given him (Jas. 1:5).

PRAYER

Father, I come to you in the name of the Lord Jesus. I desire to know you better, and through your Word, and by your Holy Spirit, be equipped to do your will in these perilous times. Please teach me how to meditate in your Word, and help me to understand the teachings of this book.

I confess that I lack wisdom, and thank you for your love in offering me some of your wisdom. Therefore I take your promise, and ask you to give me your wisdom so that I may know you. Because of your faithfulness, I receive wisdom from yourself, and thank you, in Jesus' name. Amen.

Jesus said:

And this is life eternal, that they might know thee the only true God, and Jesus Christ, whom thou hast sent (John 17:3).

Solomon wrote:

My son, if thou wilt receive my words, and hide my commandments with thee;

So that thou incline thine ear unto wisdom, and apply thine heart to understanding;

Yea, if thou criest after knowledge, and liftest up thy voice for understanding;

If thou seekest her as silver, and searchest for her as for hid treasures;

Then shalt thou understand the fear of the Lord, and find the knowledge of God (Prov. 2:1–5).

Paul wrote:

That I may know him, and the power of his resurrection, and the fellowship of his sufferings, being made comformable unto his death (Phil. 3:10).

2 *Meditation . . .*

its purpose

To know God

It is important when dealing with a single truth to ensure
it is woven into the pattern of all truth. Therefore it is
necessary before studying meditation in detail to have a
clear understanding of its purpose and its relation to other
aspects of biblical teaching. Right at the outset, therefore,
we must establish the true purpose of meditating in the
Word of God. The answer is unequivocal – to know God,
and Jesus Christ whom he hath sent, and to make them
known. In all Christian teaching it is imperative to establish beyond all doubt that the supreme focus of our thought
and study, and the deepest desire of our hearts, is a personal
knowledge of a personal God. This was the heart beat of the
apostle Paul when he wrote to the church at Colosse:

> **For this cause we also, since the day we heard it, do not
> cease to pray for you, and to desire that ye might be filled
> with the knowledge of his will in all wisdom and spiritual
> understanding;**
> **that ye might walk worthy of the Lord unto all pleasing,
> being fruitful in every good work, and increasing in the
> knowledge of God** (Col. 1:9–10).

The words of C. H. Spurgeon almost seem an understate-
ment: 'There is something exceedingly improving to the
mind in a contemplation of the Divinity . . . plunge yourself
in the Godhead's deepest sea; be lost in his immensity.'
We must be absolutely clear at this point, because no
great thoughts will come to the meditator who is not stirred
and motivated by the necessity to increase in the knowledge

of the Holy, which, in the words of Proverbs 9:10, 'is understanding'. That modern prophet, A. W. Tozer, wrote, 'We are called to an everlasting preoccupation with God.' He continued:

> The essence of idolatry is the entertainment of
> thoughts about God that are unworthy of him. The
> heaviest obligation lying upon the Christian Church
> today is to purify and elevate her concept of God until
> it is more worthy of him – and her.

Some may feel intimidated by Tozer's use of the word 'concept', so it is worthwhile asserting that a study of God, a thirst for knowledge of him, is not a quest for abstractions, nor an arid theological exercise which excels in elucidating the dull and boring, the irrelevant and impractical, but rather it is the developing of a relationship, the furtherance of a love, the deepening of a friendship that will adorn life and furnish eternity.

Paul makes it clear in 1 Corinthians 8 that without love it is impossible to be known by God or to know him. Outside a relationship of love, knowledge merely 'puffeth up', and the man who thinks he knows something, knows nothing. To know God is to love him, and to love him is to know him. You cannot love anyone you do not know. Biblical meditation increases that knowledge, and heart knowledge increases love. Obviously there cannot be a personal love for God without a personal relationship with God, so let us now deal with some of the basic truths of knowing God.

Relationship with God

The great purpose of the Lord Jesus coming to earth was to bring man back into relationship with God. Sin had separated man from God, and God in the greatness of his love desired that relationship to be restored. God had pronounced the death sentence upon sin, 'the soul that sinneth, it shall die' (Ezek. 18:4), and because 'all have sinned and come short of the glory of God' (Rom. 3:23) it required someone who was sinless to come, take the punishment for sin, so that man could be reconciled to God. This is the great message of the cross of Christ, and the Christ of the cross ... 'But God commendeth his love towards us, in that while we were yet sinners, Christ died for us' (Rom. 5:8). When we respond to the convicting work of the Holy Spirit, acknowledge and turn from our sins, believing that Jesus died for our sins, and rose again from the dead, the miracle takes place, and we are reconciled to God. What a miracle this is, in which God the Father, God the Son, and God the Holy Spirit are all operative. Jesus said, 'No man can come to me, except the Father which hath sent me draw him' (John 6:44). God draws us to Christ, who gives us eternal life: 'As thou hast given him power over all flesh, that he should give eternal life to as many as thou hast given him' (John 17:2). The Holy Spirit convicted us of sin (John 16:9) and we were renewed by the Holy Spirit (Titus 3:5). The immediate result of this new birth is that we are brought into relationship with God. 'But as many as received him, to them gave he power to become the sons of God, even to them that believe on his name' (John 1:12). A new life is imparted and we are immediately indwelt by the Holy Spirit, who witnesses with our spirit that we are children of God, assuring us of our relationship with God, who is now 'Our Father, which art in heaven.'

Eternal life is a knowledge of God

One of the many definitions of a true Christian was given by the Lord: 'And this is life eternal, that they might know thee the only true God, and Jesus Christ, whom thou hast sent' (John 17:3). Thus knowing God starts by receiving eternal life, which is given to all who believe on the Lord Jesus Christ. Obviously the knowledge of God at that time is small, but relationship has been established, and before the believer lies the glorious, exciting future of spending life and eternity in an ever increasing knowledge of the wonder and glory of God and his beloved Son, Jesus.

How about a check up?

Before proceeding further, it would be a good investment of a few minutes to have a check up. As the apostle Paul was closing his second letter to the church at Corinth, he asked all in the church to do something: 'Examine yourselves, whether ye be in the faith; prove your own selves. Know ye not your own selves, how that Jesus Christ is in you, except ye be reprobates?' (2 Cor. 13:5).

Will you do this now? You have to check yourself, but let me give you a check list of the biblical proofs of a person who has come in to a true relationship with God.

1 *A person who is a Christian knows it without any shadow of doubt.* The Holy Spirit gives the absolute assurance that we belong to God through Christ. You know.

> **The Spirit himself beareth witness with our spirit, that we are the children of God** (Romans 8:16).

> **'He that believeth on the Son of God hath the witness in himself** (1 John 5:10).

2 *A change has taken place in the life.*

> **Therefore if any man be in Christ, he is a new creature; old things are passed away; behold, all things are become new'** (2 Cor. 5:17).

3 *There is a desire to obey God.*

> **And hereby we do know that we know him, if we keep His commandments.**
> **He that saith, I know him, and keepeth not his commandments, is a liar, and the truth is not in him** (1 John 2:3–4).

4 *There is a love for other Christians.*

> **We know that we have passed from death unto life, because we love the brethren. He that loveth not his brother abideth in death** (1 John 3:14).

5 *There is a desire to know God better.*

As the hart panteth after the water brooks, so panteth my soul after thee, O God (Psalm 42:1).

6 *There is a desire to know and do the will of God.*

Not everyone that saith unto me, Lord, Lord, shall enter into the kingdom of heaven; but he that doeth the will of my Father which is in heaven (Matt. 7:21).

What is the result of your examination? Most people who have obtained this book, will, I am sure, be able to say with Paul, 'for I know whom I have believed, and am persuaded that he is able to keep that which I have committed unto him against that day' (2 Tim. 1:12). If, however, you are a reader who failed the examination, realise it is a great discovery to know where you are, or are not, with God. No one will ever call on a Saviour until he realises he has a need. If you sincerely desire to know God as your Father, and Jesus Christ as your Lord, obey the Word of God as it encourages you to do the following:

Acknowledge your need

Agree with what the Bible says about you,

All we like sheep have gone astray, we have turned every one to his own way (Isa. 53:6).

For all have sinned and come short of the glory of God (Rom. 3:23).

Take the cry of the publican, 'God be merciful to me, a sinner' (Luke 18:13). If you have one good word to say for yourself, you are not a candidate for God's salvation, for he is only the Saviour of sinners.

But we are all as an unclean thing, and all our righteousnesses are as filthy rags; and we all do fade as a leaf; and our iniquities, like the wind, have taken us away (Isa. 64:6).

Look to the Lord Jesus

He is the only Saviour. He is the only way to God. He said:

I am the way, the truth, and the life; no man cometh unto the Father but by me (John 14:6).

Look unto me, and be ye saved, all the ends of the earth; for I am God, and there is none else (Isa. 45:22).

Believe in Him

Believe that which is true, that he loves you, he died for you, he took the punishment for your sins, that he, Jesus, 'died for our sins according to the Scriptures; and that he was buried, and that he rose again the third day according to the Scriptures' (1 Cor. 15:3–4).

Receive him as your Saviour and Lord

Having acknowledged your sin, and repented, believing that he died for you and rose again, ask him to come into your life, yielding it totally to his Lordship.

But as many as received him, to them gave he power to become the sons of God, even to them that believe on his name (John 1:12).

Confess him as Lord

That if thou shalt confess with thy mouth the Lord Jesus, and shalt believe in thine heart that God hath raised him from the dead, thou shalt be saved.
  For with the heart man believeth unto righteousness; and with the mouth confession is made unto salvation (Rom. 10:9–10).

Now look at the record

And this is the record that God hath given to us eternal life, and this life is in his Son.

He that hath the Son hath life; he that hath not the Son of God hath not life (1 John 5:11–12).

APPLICATION

If you have never before accepted the Lord Jesus as your Saviour and Lord; if your profession of faith has only been nominal and you did not pass the test of examining yourself whether you are 'in the faith'; and if you really desire to have a relationship with God, pray now.

PRAYER

O God, I come to you, acknowledging I am a sinner, and I am ready now to repent of my sin, to turn from sin. God have mercy on me, a sinner. I believe that the Lord Jesus died on the cross for my sins, and that he rose again from the dead. I ask you now, Lord Jesus, to save me, and I receive you as my own Saviour. I yield all of my life to you. I confess with my mouth that you are Christ Jesus my Lord, and that you have given me eternal life. I believe I am now indwelt by your Holy Spirit, and that you, O God, are now my Father. Thank you. I acknowledge it is all because of your mercy and grace. Amen.

If you have just become a Christian, tell someone about it. Get committed to and involved with a Bible believing church. Continue to read this book and apply its teachings, which will enable you to increase in the knowledge of God.

God bless you.

For ever, O Lord, thy word is settled in heaven (Ps. 119:89).

I will worship toward thy holy temple, and praise thy name for thy lovingkindness and for thy truth; for thou hast magnified thy word above all thy name (Ps. 138:2).

Buy the truth, and sell it not; also wisdom, and instruction and understanding (Prov. 23:23).

. . . and he saith unto me, These are the true sayings of God Rev. 19:9).

3 *Meditation . . .*

The Bible

The Bible meditator must be one who affirms that God has spoken to man, and that the Bible is a record of what he has said. This is a basic principle of knowing God. It has been the undermining of the Bible as the revealed word of God that has erroded the necessity which men once felt to consult it, and wrecked those devotional habits, particularly meditation, that deepen a love for God's Word, and strengthen the desire to read and obey it.

The Bible meditator also acknowledges that God's Word is truth, and that through that truth God communicates his character, his commands, his promises and his instructions. Acquiring the knowledge of God is not meant to be merely fulfilling one of the rules of being a Christian. If getting to know God is done out of obligation and duty, it will produce little, but if we desire to know God because we love him, it will produce much. David, with his great love for God, cries out in Psalm 31:23: 'O love the Lord, all ye his saints.' Loving God is not initially a thing of the emotions but of the will. Jesus said, 'Love the Lord your God with all your heart and with all your soul.' We choose to love God.

Love for God is evidenced in various ways. *Firstly*, it is shown by our obedience. Jesus said to his disciples, 'If ye love me; keep my commandments' (John 14:15).

Secondly, our love is shown by love for his Word. You cannot separate a person from their voice. If you love a person, you will love their voice, and God's Word is his voice to us. Over the past twenty years, I have ministered in many places in different parts of the world. This has necessitated my being away from home for periods ranging from a few days to a few months. When I receive letters from my wife I do not say to myself, 'Campbell, one of the rules of being a good husband is that you should always read her letters.' No, I eagerly read and reread them. Why? I just happen to love the author, so reading is a pleasure.

Years ago I was staying in a friend's home in Sydney, Australia. I had been away from home for several months and my friend asked me when I had last spoken to Shelagh, my wife. I told him the last time I spoke to her was the day I left home. He picked up the telephone and invited me to phone my home in England. After a few moments I heard a voice, and there were flutterings in my heart. Why? I couldn't see her, I couldn't touch her, but I heard the voice. I loved the voice because I loved her.

Peter wrote, 'Whom having not seen, ye love; though now ye see him not, yet believing, ye rejoice with joy unspeakable, and full of glory' (1 Pet. 1:8). David's love for God was also expressed in his love for his Word. 'Therefore I love thy commandments above gold, yea above fine gold . . . O how love I thy law! it is my meditation all the day (Ps. 119:127, 97).

Thirdly, our love for God is shown in our love for one another. Someone has said that if you want to know how much you love God, think of the Christian you love least, and you have the answer. As John wrote, 'If a man say, I love God, and hateth his brother, he is a liar; for he that loveth not his brother whom he hath seen, how can he love God whom he hath not seen?' (1 John 4:20).

You cannot love what you do not appreciate

One of the purposes of this book is that we will all have a greater love for God and appreciation of his Word. Beyond all the works of creation and providence by which God has made himself known, he has exalted his name and his Word. 'Thou hast magnified thy Word above all thy name' (Ps. 138:2), or as the New International version, 'For you have exalted above all things your name and your Word.'

Calvin translated it, 'Thou hast magnified thy name above all things by thy Word,' and Martin Luther's version, 'Thou hast made thy name glorious above all through thy Word.' What a Word this is! Through its pages we can know the eternal God and his beloved Son Jesus. We can know the will of God for our lives. We can be brought into the plans and purposes of God. It reveals to us the history of the past, power for the present, and plans for the future. May we all come to the place where we can truly proclaim with David, 'O how love I thy law!' Then it will not be difficult to come to the place where we will also say, 'I meditate on it all day long.'

It is the book of books

Of the millions of books in the world, what a privilege it is to have the greatest of them all, the Bible. The word 'Bible' comes from a Greek word which means the inner bark of the papyrus plant, a substance from which was obtained the material which took the place of writing paper in ancient times. It is a book from God, about God. It is not like any other book ever written. It was written by men who heard the voice of God and wrote what they were inspired to write by the Holy Spirit.

For the prophecy came not in old time by the will of man; but holy men of God spake as they were moved by the Holy Ghost (2 Pet. 1:21).

Paul wrote to Timothy, 'all scripture is God breathed' (2 Tim. 3:16 (NIV).

The Bible was written over a period of 1500 years, by forty different authors of varying backgrounds. Moses, who wrote the first five books, was adopted by the daughter of the greatest king of his time, and learned the knowledge available in one of the most civilised and cultured nations known to history – a nation with knowledge of arts and crafts which exceeded most future generations. On the other hand, other authors like Peter and John were lowly born, unlettered fishermen. Daniel was a statesman of royal birth, holding high office in the kingdom of Babylon; Amos was a herdsman; David was a warrior king, and a skilled musician and poet. Solomon, his son, was a powerful monarch, whose wealth and wisdom were renowned far beyond his own nation. Paul was a highly educated Pharisee, a theologian of his day, tutored by the finest teachers; while Matthew was a tax collector under the Roman government; and Luke, a physician. What a variety of writers, yet all were moved by the same divine Spirit, irrespective of background, culture or education.

Because this book is God breathed, it has power to convict and convert, to sanctify and edify. It has been called 'the mirror of the author' because it reveals, unveils, magnifies and glorifies him from whom it originally came. Because it is God breathed it has life. While J. B. Phillips was translating the New Testament he described the experience thus: 'Although I did my utmost to preserve an emotional detatchment, I found again and again that the material under my hands was strangely alive; it spoke to my condition in the most uncanny way.'

The Bible enables us to establish a relationship with God, it is a signpost to the Lord Jesus. Its teachings equip us for the circumstances and difficulties of life. It is a guide for our conduct, showing man how he can live in the realm of greatest blessing and fulfillment. It is not only good literature, not only a history of the nation of Israel, not only a book of theological content – it is the *living word* of *the living God.*

The miracle of its preservation

No book ever written has had such opposition to its translation and publication. To many it has been the most loved book, to others the most hated. Men such as Voltaire have prophesied its destruction. He said, 'in one hundred years the book will be forgotten', and as is commonly known, one hundred years later Voltaire's house was the headquarters of the Geneva Bible Society. Why has it survived when each

20

era brings renewed efforts to stamp it out? Why, in spite of all the attacks by atheistic, humanistic and other philosophies, does it remain one of the world's best sellers? The answer is not only is it God breathed, but it is also God preserved. Jesus said, 'heaven and earth shall pass away, but my words shall never pass away' (Matt. 24:35).

Its translations and translators

We should be grateful to God for all his faithful servants down through the centuries who have been used to translate the Scriptures so that we can have the book of books in our homes and in our hands. We can thank him for Jerome, who spent twenty years in the fourth century translating the Word into Latin. This Latin Vulgate became the Church's official version.

Following the Reformation it was obvious that there was a need to translate Scripture into the national languages. Luther's version was adopted by the German Lutheran Churches. Although there had been several attempts to translate parts of the Bible into English, notably by the Venerable Bede in the seventh century, King Alfred in the ninth century, and Wycliffe in the fourteenth century, it was not until 1526 that the first New Testament was printed in English, through the efforts of William Tyndale. In 1535 Coverdale published the first full Bible in English. Other versions followed before the publication of the Authorised, or King James version in 1611. In 1881, a Revised Version was produced, based on a rendering from the original text. Then other versions came forth such as the Revised Standard Version, the New English Bible and Todays English Version. The purpose of some of these translations was to use more modern language in the contemporary idiom.

The twentieth century has produced more translations than any other. In 1903, R. T. Weymouth produced his New Testament in Modern Speech. In 1913, James Moffatt: A New Translation of the Bible. In 1927, E. J. Godspeeds the Complete Bible. In 1944, Ronald Knox's Holy Bible. In

1946, the Revised Standard Version. In 1950, the New World Translation. In 1958, the Amplified Bible, also J. B. Phillip's the New Testament in Modern English. In 1961, the New English Bible. In 1966, the Jerusalem Bible, also in 1966, Todays English Version produced by the American Bible Society. In 1971, Kenneth Taylor's the Living Bible, and in 1978, the New International Version.

Some of these translations were produced by one man, others by a group of scholars. One of the reasons for the translations was a concern to keep the idiom and general force and meaning as closely as possible to the original text, but in language easily understood by the reader.

The price paid

Spare a thought for the price men paid. John Wycliffe, who was a lecturer at Oxford, a Member of Parliament, and Rector of Lutterworth, was viciously attacked for his work of translation. He was accused of being 'a pestilent wretch, the son of the old serpent, the forerunner of the antichrist'. Although he died from natural causes, many of the readers of his translation were burned to death with the copies around their necks. Men and women were executed for teaching their children from the Bible. His translation was banned and those who possessed it were hunted down like wild beasts. Tyndale copies were seized and publicly burned. Alluding to this he remarked, 'In burning the New Testament they do none other things than I looked for. No more shall they do it, if they burn me alive also.' Later this actually happened and Tyndale was martyred by being burned alive.

Others also paid the supreme price. After the brief seven years' reign of Edward VI ensued the five dark years of the reign of 'Bloody Mary', during which time John Rogers, who translated a Bible known as Matthews Bible was martyred, and others also who stood for Bible truth such as Latimer, Ridley and Cranmer. Others had to flee the country, and about all these we could borrow the words from Hebrews 11:38, '. . . of whom the world was not worthy'.

But far above all, let us worship and praise our God for our precious, blessed Lord Jesus the living Word, who was mocked, rejected, scourged, spat upon, crowned with thorns and crucified that we might not only have the Word in our hands but the Word in our hearts, indwelt by his very life. He died, rose again, and ascended to the right hand of God the Father, not only that we could have a book in our hands called the New Testament, but that experientially we might know and live in a New Covenant relationship with him, the living Word.

APPLICATION

Does your life demonstrate that you love God:
(a) *By your obedience?*
   If not, confess your sin of disobedience and tell the Lord you are now going to obey him.

(b) *By your love for his Word?*
   If not, tell him you are willing and ready for change, and that you intend to apply the teachings of this book, in order to know him better.

(c) *By your love for others?*
   If not, confess these things to the Lord, make restitution where necessary and apply the Lord's teaching of Matthew 5:44, and pray his blessing on these people.

PRAYER

Father, I thank thee for thy Word. I thank thee, and acknowledge it is your Word, the Word of God. Thank you for those you inspired to write it, and for their obedience. Thank you for all who contributed to its translation, so that I may have it in my hands today. Thank you for preserving it, in spite of all efforts to destroy it, and help me, please, Lord, to have an ever increasing appreciation of it. Lord Jesus, thank you for coming to be the living Word, and for the great price you paid to enable me to know you. Amen.

This know also, that in the last days perilous times shall come.

For men shall be lovers of their own selves, covetous, boasters, proud, blasphemers, disobedient to parents, unthankful, unholy,

Without natural affection, trucebreakers, false accusers, incontinent, fierce, despisers of those that are good,

Traitors, heady, highminded, lovers of pleasures more than lovers of God;

Having a form of godliness, but denying the power thereof: from such turn away . . .

But evil men and seducers shall wax worse and worse, deceiving, and being deceived.

But continue thou in the things which thou hast learned and has been assured of, knowing of whom thou hast learned them.

And that from a child thou hast known the holy scriptures, which are able to make thee wise unto salvation through faith which is in Christ Jesus.

All scripture is given by inspiration of God, and is profitable for doctrine, for reproof, for correction, for instruction in righteousness;

That the man of God may be perfect, throughly furnished unto all good works (2 Tim. 3:1–5; 13–17).

4 *Meditation . . .*

desire for

We must grow up

As never before, it is essential for every Christian to examine his attitude to the Word of God and the development of his knowledge of God through its contents. At a great price, as we have seen in the previous chapter, this treasure has been given to us, that we might be a people of the Word of God.

> **For God who commanded the light to shine out of darkness, hath shined in our hearts, to give the light of knowledge of the glory of God in the face of Jesus Christ.**
> **But we have this treasure in earthen vessels, that the excellency of the power may be of God, and not of us** (2 Cor. 4:6–7).

Having shone in our hearts through 'the light of the glorious gospel', we can continually receive more light, more treasure, through the knowledge of God and the Lord Jesus.

The verses with which the chapter begins were written by the apostle Paul, while awaiting his executioners. In his final letter to Timothy, he emphasises the importance of the Word of God in the darkness of the 'last days'. We are now living in this context – this is a word to you and to me. If we are going to stand we must be strong, and that strength comes from God and through a knowledge of him. Daniel wrote:

> **. . . the people that know their God shall be strong and do exploits, and they that understand among the people shall instruct many** (Dan. 11:32–3).

Paul reminded his readers that the Scriptures were

written for our learning. It could be argued that so much of the Bible is read while so little is learned. T. S. Eliot's assessment of twentieth century man was, 'They have a knowledge of words but not of *the* Word.' Therefore let us note carefully and prayerfully the exhortation of Paul for the last days:

(a) We must be men and women of the Word if we are to be alert to deceit and the deceiver.

(b) We must continue in the Word and hold it fast if we are to be able to commit it to others.

(c) We must learn from it and give ourselves to meditation and study, not in a careless, routine dominated manner, but with the spirit of a willing learner, dependent on the Spirit of God, our great teacher.

(d) We must realise afresh that everything in the Bible is profitable, and that the 'favourite book' and 'just a few verses' syndromes are not concomitant with the desire to be godly.

(e) We must agree with Paul that a knowledge of God through the Word will equip us for ministry in the name of the Lord, and that there is no ministry outside a love for the Word of God.

(f) Only with such a view of Scripture could Timothy obey Paul's injunction to 'preach the Word . . . reprove, rebuke, exhort'.

We must become people of the Word, who study to show ourselves approved to God, workmen who need not be ashamed. Bible meditation is one of the essential means that God is seeking to restore to make us people who not only know *that* God has spoken, but also *what* he has spoken.

The purpose of this, and the succeeding chapters, is not only to increase our desire to be people of the Word, but the result of that desire will be a commitment of our lives to know him who is the living Word through the written Word. The assessment of our spiritual maturity is determined by the answer to the question, 'How well do I know God?' Too many Christians are living in unnecessary stages of immaturity. Jesus said, 'Ye do err, not knowing the scriptures, nor the power of God' (Matt. 22:29); and the apostle Paul, writing to the church at Corinth and admonishing them for their lack of growth, said:

And I, brethren, could not speak unto you as unto spiritual, but as unto carnal, even as unto babes in Christ.

I have fed you with milk, and not with meat: for hitherto ye were not able to bear it, neither yet now are ye able.

For ye are yet carnal: for whereas there is among you envying, and strife, and divisions, are ye not carnal, and walk as men? (1 Cor. 3:1–3).

Again, the writer to the Hebrews has the same complaint and heartbreak:

For when for the time ye ought to be teachers, ye have need that one teach you again which be the first principles of the oracles of God; and are become such as have need of milk, and not of strong meat.

For everyone that useth milk is unskilful in the word of righteousness; for he is a babe.

But strong meat belongeth to them that are of full age, even those who by reason of use, have their senses exercised to discern both good and evil (Heb. 5:12–14).

How tragic it is in the physical realm to see an adult who has never grown mentally but still behaves like a babe and needs a babe's attention. Boreham, in one of his books, shares one of his boyhood experiences. While living in an aunt's home, he noticed a bedroom door which was continually locked. With a boy's curiosity he hid in a closet in the corridor and waited. Later his aunt came, unlocked the door, and he saw lying on the bed a boy in his teens with the mind of a child. His heart was moved as he watched his aunt take the boy in her arms and cry, 'I have loved you all these years, yet you have never known me.' How long have we known the Lord? How well do we know him? May we be saved from giving him heartbreak.

We will not grow without continual revelation of God and

from God through his Word. Meditation is one of the means of receiving such revelation.

APPLICATION

Do you believe your spiritual growth is commensurate with the time you have known God?

Have you neglected the means of growth? What adjustments do you believe are necessary in your life to correct this? List them here:

PRAYER

Father, thank you for all that you have taught me of yourself, but I long to know you better. Please forgive me where I have neglected my spiritual growth, through laziness, or being too busy with other things, or because of coldness of heart. I desire to be a mature Christian. I do not want to disappoint you and give you heartache. Help me, please, to be disciplined, and to continue in your Word, and take me beyond the milk stage to enable me to take the meat of the Word, in Jesus' name. Amen.

Then said they unto him, What shall we do, that we might work the works of God?

Jesus answered and said unto them, This is the work of God, that ye believe on him whom he hath sent.

They said therefore unto him, What sign shewest thou then, that we may see, and believe thee? what dost thou work?

Our fathers did eat manna in the desert; as it is written, He gave them bread from heaven to eat.

Then Jesus said unto them, Verily, verily, I say unto you, Moses gave you not that bread from heaven; but my Father giveth you the true bread from heaven.

For the bread of God is he which cometh down from heaven, and giveth life unto the world.

Then said they unto him, Lord, evermore give us this bread.

And Jesus said unto them, I am the bread of life; he that cometh to me shall never hunger; and he that believeth on me shall never thirst (John 6:28–35).

5 *Meditation . . .*

requirements for (1)

Life out of death

**But thou Bethlehem Ephratah, though thou be little among
the thousands of Judah, yet out of thee shall he come forth
unto me that is to be ruler in Israel; whose goings forth
have been from of old, from everlasting** (Mic. 5:2).

It was the fulfilment of this prophecy, the birth of Jesus
Christ the Son of God, that made Bethlehem historic among
all the places of the world. We are going to take the words
of the shepherds on our lips: 'Let us now go to Bethlehem.'
We are going to practise some 'spiritualising' of certain
scriptures which refer to events in Bethlehem, not in order
to (in the words of Spurgeon) 'show the superfine critics
that everybody does not worship the golden image which
they have set up', but to illustrate some of the marks of a
meditator, some of the characteristics of those who would
feed from the Word of God.

Bethlehem means 'the house of bread'. It was also known
as Ephratah, meaning 'fruitfulness', and sometimes it is
referred to as Bethelehem-Judah; Judah, of course, meaning 'praise'. It should be our desire to be Bethlehemites, as
it were; men and women of the house of bread, feeding on
the Word of God so that we are fruitful in every good work
and among those who continually praise God.

Bethlehem . . . the place of life

**Let us know go even unto Bethlehem, and see this thing
which is come to pass, which the Lord hath made known
unto us** (Luke 2:15).

The 'thing' that had happened was the birth of a Saviour, Christ the Lord – news of great joy for all people. It is this event that sets forth the most fundamental, distinctive and amazing Christian claim – that at Bethlehem, God became man in the person of his Son, Jesus.

There is no greater truth, there is no deeper mystery, than the incarnation, which, in bold type, writes large the unfathomable grace of God as it is manifested in his Son, Jesus, who became poor for our sakes, and became obedient to death, even the death of the cross. Perhaps the clearest expression of this truth is to be found in the opening chapter of John's gospel, where the Son of God is established as the revelation of the divine Word. This Word is the giver of life and light; it is eternal and divine; it is the revelation of the heart of God and living evidence that God so loved the world. Mystery of mysteries, at Bethlehem 'the Word became flesh' and actually lived among us for a while! At Bethlehem began the manifestation of God to men through Jesus, because 'the only begotten Son, which is the bosom of the Father, he hath declared him'.

What better place than 'the house of bread' for Jesus Christ, the living Word, to begin his life; Jesus who said of himself, 'I am the bread of life; he that cometh to me shall never hunger' (John 6:35). Meditation is feeding on Christ, inwardly receiving the Word that gives a greater knowledge of God and the experience related by St Bernard:

> We taste thee, O thou living Word,
> And long to feed upon thee still.
> We drink of thee the fountain-head,
> And thirst our souls from thee to fill.

The Bethlehemite is therefore someone who glories in the fact of the incarnation and, through personal salvation, praises God for the purposes that were realised in the birth, life and death of the God-man. Furthermore, the true Bethlehemite is one whose desire for God is reflected in his appetite for the Word, his avowed intention never to leave the house of bread. In the words of William Williams, such a one cries,

Bread of heaven, feed me till I want no more.

You will remember in the story in the book of Ruth, that it was when Elimilech, Naomi, and their two sons left Bethlehem that loss and sadness came to them. Only when Naomi decided to return to Bethlehem, the house of bread, was blessing restored.

Bethlehem . . . the place of death

Bethlehem became a significant landmark in the life of Jacob. We read the story in Genesis 35. Jacob's sons had been involved in wiping out most of the population of a city called Shechem, because the prince of Shechem had seduced their sister, Dinah. Jacob was fearful for his life, knowing that news of this incident would quickly carry to surrounding cities. God spoke to Jacob and told him to return with his family to Bethel, that place where he had that initial meeting with God, and vowed, 'The Lord shall be my God' (Gen. 28:21). Having been to Bethel, they made their way towards Bethlehem. Rachel, Jacob's wife, whom he loved so deeply, was about to give birth to her second child, and we take up the story from there . . .

> **And they journeyed from Bethel, and there was but a little way to come to Ephrath; and Rachel travailed, and she had hard labour.**
> **And it came to pass when she was in hard labour, that the midwife said unto her, Fear not; thou shalt have this son also.**
> **And it came to pass, as her soul was in departing, (for she died,) that she called his name Benoni; but his father called him Benjamin.**
> **And Rachel died, and was buried in the way to Ephrath, which is Bethlehem.**
> **And Jacob set a pillar upon her grave; that is the pillar of Rachel's grave unto this day.**
> **And Israel journeyed . . .** (Gen. 35:15–21).

As well as illustrative truth for the meditator, what an apposite picture this is of the Christ who would come to

Bethlehem. Rachel said, 'call him Benoni', which means 'son of my sorrow', but Jacob called him Benjamin, which means 'son of the right hand'. Before Jesus again became 'Son of the right hand' he had to become 'the Son of my sorrow'.

Man of sorrows what a name.
For the Son of man who came,
Ruined sinner to reclaim.
Hallelujah, what a Saviour.

Lifted up was he to die,
It is finished was his cry,
Now in heaven exalted high.
Hallelujah, what a Saviour

For Jacob, Bethlehem was the place where he buried that which was dearest to him. So it is for every true 'Bethlehemite' – that which is dearest and best to us must go to the place of death and burial, so that the call of God comes before the call of men. Everything which would interfere with our being people of God and knowing God, must be taken to the cross, so that truly we will 'seek first the kingdom of God, and his righteousness'. As this was a landmark in Jacob's life, so it can be in yours. Jacob erected a pillar at this place of death, but having done so, it is recorded that Israel journeyed on – Israel – that name given to him by God 'as a prince hast thou power with God, and with men, and hast prevailed' (Gen. 32:28). We can know little of the power of God, little of prevailing, little of knowing God, until in our hearts we have come to that place of death, so that we know the experience of true spiritual living.

There is a divine principle that life comes from death. Jesus said, 'Verily, verily, I say unto you, Except a corn of wheat fall into the ground and die, it abideth alone; but if it die it bringeth forth much fruit' (John 12:24). Sometimes we hold on to things not knowing how we could live without them, and yet realising they have a place in our life they should not have, and all the time the Lord wants to give us something better.

I remember when one of my daughters was about three years old, she came running into the room with a nice, shining pepper shaker in her hand. It looked so attractive, but I knew something she did not know; there was something inside which could hurt her if it got in her eyes. Her brother also saw it and went to snatch it out of her hand, but I stopped him. There happened to be a piece of chocolate on the table, so I took a piece and held it out to the child. When she saw it she put her hand out to take it, and as she did so I took the pepper shaker from her other hand. When God asks us to take anything to the place of death, it is because he knows it will hurt us if we keep it, and he wants to give us something better.

The Lord does not want us to have anything in our lives which comes before him. When ministering in New Zealand some years ago, a young lady came to me at the end of a service. She had been weeping and seemed troubled. She told me that in the service the Lord had shown her there was something in her life that had a place it shouldn't have. I asked her what it was, and to my amazement she said, 'A horse.' Jill's parents were farmers, and she had a very fine horse and was a very accomplished rider. She told me the Lord had told her to sell it and give the proceeds to some missionaries.

I encouraged her to obey God, knowing that she would be blessed and the Lord would be pleased. Sometime later, I received a long letter from her, telling me what had happened. When she went home, she put an advert in the paper announcing the sale of the horse. She did not receive any replies, so decided she would put it up for sale at the annual Agricultural Fair in a town nearby. The day came and she took her lovely horse to the auction. She sat waiting her turn to ride her horse around the sales ring, and was disappointed at the low price horses were fetching that day. Her turn came, and as she rode her horse around before the would-be purchasers, the bids went higher, and higher till the horse was sold for a very good price. She asked the auctioneer if he would ask the new owner to contact her, so that she could tell him what the horse liked and disliked. The parting was very sad, but she had chosen to obey God. As she was waiting, her uncle came to her and said, 'Jill, put the horse in the truck.' She said, 'No, uncle. I have just sold it.' He said, 'I know. I have just bought it. No, that's not quite accurate, your grandmother has bought it. When she heard what the Lord had told you to do, she said, "I will buy it", but the Lord told her to let you go all the way to the sale.' Later that day Jill saw her grandmother who said, 'Jill, here is the money for the horse to send to the missionaries, and Jill, here is the horse. I give it back to you.' Although Jill loved that horse, it never had the same place in her life again. It is a reminder of the story of Abraham's obedience in taking Isaac to Mount Moriah to offer him to the Lord. Truly Isaac was offered, but Abraham walked down the mountain again with him.

The Lord desires and deserves one place in our lives — *first* place.

APPLICATION

Is there anything in your life which interferes with the Lord Jesus being first? If there is, this will also interfere with you being a 'Bethlehemite', a person of the Word, and a 'Ephrathite', a fruitful Christian. If there is anyone or anything which has a greater priority than the Lord, yield it totally to the Lord. Why not write these things down here, and surrender each to him.

PRAYER

Father, I really want to be a person of the house of bread. I want to be a fruitful Christian and a praising Christian. I yield everything to you, dear Lord. I choose that you should be *first* in my life, that I love you more than anyone or anything. I yield myself to you, knowing that what I commit, you receive, and what you receive, you use and bless. Thank you for your love in showing me things that have had a place in my life they should not have had. I know, and thank you, that you love me. Amen.

And the Lord said unto Samuel, how long wilt thou mourn for Saul, seeing I have rejected him from reigning over Israel? fill thine horn with oil, and go, I will send thee to Jesse the Bethlehemite: for I have provided me a king among his sons.

And Samuel said, How can I go? if Saul hear it, he will kill me. And the Lord said, take an heifer with thee, and say, I am come to sacrifice to the Lord.

And call Jesse to the sacrifice, and I will show thee what thou shalt do; and thou shalt anoint unto me him whom I name unto thee.

And Samuel did that which the Lord spake, and came to Bethlehem. And the elders of the town trembled at his coming, and said, Comest thou peaceably?

And he said, Peaceably: I am come to sacrifice unto the Lord: sanctify yourselves, and come with me to the sacrifice. And he sanctified Jesse and his sons, and called them to the sacrifice.

And it came to pass, when they were come, that he looked on Eliab, and said, Surely the Lord's anointed is before him.

But the Lord said unto Samuel, Look not on his countenance, or on the height of his stature; because I have refused him: for the Lord seeth not as man seeth; for man looketh on the outward appearance, but the Lord looketh on the heart . . .

And Samuel said unto Jesse, Are here all thy children? And he said, There remaineth yet the youngest, and behold, he keepeth the sheep. And Samuel said unto Jesse, Send and fetch him: for we will not sit down till he come hither.

And he sent, and brought him in. Now he was ruddy, and withal of a beautiful countenance, and goodly to look to. And the Lord said, Arise, anoint him: for this is he.

Then Samuel took the horn of oil, and anointed him in the midst of his brethren: and the spirit of the Lord came upon David from that day forward. So Samuel rose up, and went to Ramah. . . .

Then answered one of the servants, and said, Behold, I have seen a son of Jesse the Bethlehemite, that is cunning in playing, and a mighty valiant man, and a man of war, and prudent in matters, and a comely person, and the Lord is with him (1 Sam. 16:1–7, 11–13, 18).

6 Meditation . . .

requirements for (2)

The 'Bethlehemite'

Again we go to Bethlehem to learn further lessons, so that we might be better prepared to be meditators in the Word of God. The story is taken from 1 Samuel 16, with its background of King Saul, who had been such a disappointment of God and to the prophet Samuel. Samuel was heartbroken because Saul had forfeited the right to rule over Israel through deliberate disobedience to clear instructions from God. At this time the word of the Lord comes to Samuel bringing the answer for the situation.

How long will you mourn?

When God is wanting to do new things, it is unprofitable to mourn over past failures. Where there have been failures and sin, let us confess and forsake them and accept God's challenge to become men and women of the Word of God. You may be conscious of failure in past years to get to know God through His Word, but thank God for *now*. Things can be different with a determination to follow on to know the Lord:

> **. . . forgetting those things which are behind, and reaching forth unto those things which are before, I press toward the mark for the prize of the high calling of God in Christ Jesus** (Phil. 3:13–14).

You will be a 'Bethlehemite' as you allow the Spirit of God to deal with the past and release you into the present plan of God for your enrichment in the house of bread.

39

Fill your horn with oil and go ... to Bethlehem

The answer to the leadership question was going to be found at Bethlehem, but Samuel is told to go there with the oil. Oil is one of the emblems used in Scripture for the Holy Spirit, without whose help we cannot be spiritual Bethlehemites. How wonderful to have the author of the Word with us and in us, helping us to meditate on and understand the Scriptures. The greatest Bible school in the world is the Holy Spirit Bible School ... open 24 hours a day ... the library of sixty-six books accessible ... the teacher always available. Jesus said of him:

> **Howbeit when he, the Spirit of truth, is come, he will guide you in to all truth: for he shall not speak of himself; but whatsoever he shall hear, that shall he speak: and he will show you things to come.**
> **He shall glorify me: for he shall receive of mine, and shall show it unto you** (John 16:13–14).

Never go to Bethlehem without the oil. 'Lean not unto thine own understanding,' Solomon counsels us. Spiritual truth can only be spiritually discerned and understood. When our lives are like that horn, open-ended to heaven, filled with the Holy Spirit, then we will know what it is to be taught of the Lord, to be Bethlehemites in the house of bread.

I have provided a king

For Samuel, Bethlehem was the place where he would discover the man of God's choice to rule Israel. Our discovery in the Word will be that all things have been provided in the Son of God's choice, and that not only as he provided but he has provided abundantly.

I will show thee what thou shalt do

Before going to Bethlehem, Samuel had received the promise of revelation, but it was only as he obeyed God and went there that the revelation itself was revealed. Thank God for every promise he has given us that he will show us what to do; but that revelation is given to us mainly through the Word of God, as we go to it, read it, study it and meditate upon it. God is as willing to guide us as he was to guide Samuel. Many Christians find divine guidance a problem, but it is mainly a self-inflicted problem. There is a danger of being lost on a journey if you do not read the map, of being shipwrecked without sailing according to the chart, of failing examinations because the text books were not read, and of missing the will of God because of a failure to discover it through his Word. The revelation of the will of God is the experience of the true Bethlehemite.

Samuel did that which the Lord spake

He went to Bethlehem. The result of his obedience meant blessing to a whole nation because they received the king of God's choice. Furthermore, obedience resulted in the fulfilling of his own ministry as a prophet. Just think of the multitude of people and circumstances that can be blessed if we go to God's Word and obey it. Without such obedience, in spite of all the good intentions in the world, there will not be a fulfilling of your own ministry and function in the Body of Christ. The diary of the true Bethlehemite will also be punctuated by the same entry, 'he or she did that which the Lord spake'.

Man looks on the outward appearance; the Lord looks on the heart

When Samuel arrived in Bethlehem, he called together Jesse and his sons and began to look at them. The first son to come was Eliab, a tall, good looking man, no doubt similar in many ways to King Saul. One can understand Samuel's reaction: 'Surely, the Lord's anointed is before me.' But here at Bethlehem God would not allow his servant to make a mistake and be deceived by outward appearance. God looks on hearts. What a comfort this is. When we choose to do the will of God, and as Bethlehemites let his

Word be our guide, we will not judge by outward appearance, because we will be cognizant of God's standards and God's views. The Lord said to Samuel, 'I have refused him: for the Lord seeth not as man seeth; for man looketh on the outward appearance, but the Lord looketh on the heart.'

The house of bread is a place of protection from misguided assessments and wrong judgments, because it is the place of dependence on the judgments of God.

Arise, anoint him: this is he

To Samuel's amazement, all of Jesse's sons passed before him and God had not selected any. 'Are here all thy children?' he asks the father. 'There remaineth yet the youngest, and behold, he keepeth the sheep,' replied Jesse – what a wonderful place to find a shepherd for Israel! According to some Jewish tradition, David was an illegitimate son, 'in sin did my mother conceive me', and thus he was despised by some of his brethren. 'Send and fetch him; for we will not sit down till he come,' said Samuel. David was brought in and God said, 'Arise, anoint him: for this is he.'

The anointing was necessary for God's chosen Bethlehemite. That anointing signified that he was the man of God's choice, with the power of God available by the Spirit to fulfil that task for the glory of God. The same Holy Spirit who was going to teach David and guide him is given to us. John wrote:

> . . . the anointing which ye have received of him abideth in you, and ye need not that any man teach you: but as the same anointing teacheth you of all things, and is truth, and is no lie, and even as it hath taught you, ye shall abide in him (1 John 2:27).

The characteristics of a Bethlehemite

Later in the story we read that Saul, who had rejected God, was going through times of deep trouble, and his servants suggested to him that a good musician might soothe him in his troubles. He was told of the skills and ability of a young man called David, 'a son of Jesse, the Bethlehemite'. The description given of David is most interesting, as it is the description of all who are true spiritual Bethlehemites – meditating in the Word and joyously obeying it. This is what they said of him:

1. *A cunning player*
The word 'cunning' simply means that he was skilled in playing the harp, his musical instrument used to worship God. The more we read and meditate on the Word, the more skilful we will become in praising and worshipping God, thus fulfilling our first priority: 'Thou shalt worship the Lord thy God with all thine heart, and him only shalt thou serve.'

2. *A mighty valiant man*
The Word will make us 'strong in the Lord and in the power of his might'. Remember again Daniel 11:32, 'The people that know their God shall be strong and do exploits.'

3. *A man of war*
Every Christian is engaged in a battle against the world, the flesh, and the devil, 'wrestling against principalities, against powers, against the rulers of the darkness of this world, against spiritual wickedness in high places' (Eph. 6:12). In these days the battle is getting fiercer and we need to be men of war who know how to take 'the sword of the Spirit, which is the Word of God' (Eph. 6:17).

4. *Prudent in matters.*
This meant that David had intelligent understanding. Paul exhorts us in Ephesians 5:17, 'Wherefore be not unwise, but understanding what the will of the Lord is.' There is no understanding of that will without a knowledge of the Word of God.

5. *A comely person.*

This lovely expression means that he was well balanced. There is a danger in Christian experience of becoming unbalanced unless we are grounded in the Word. There are two dangers regarding truth: one is the underemphasis of truth, and the other is the overemphasis of truth. Where there is an overemphasis you will find the person is always talking about it. The 'Bethlehemite' will be a well balanced person, one whose life is focused on the centrality of Christ. It is impossible to overemphasise him!

6. *The Lord is with him.*

This was always the experience of the men and women in Scripture who knew God and knew his Word – there was the evidence of God being with them and working with them. It was evident that the blessing of the Lord was on the life of David. John Wesley used to say, 'best of all, God is with us'.

7. *A source of refreshment.*

It is recorded that 'David took an harp, and played with his hand; so Saul was refreshed, and was well.' A meditator will be a refreshment, sharing today's bread and not those scraps which have been kept on ice in the spiritual deep-freeze.

APPLICATION

Check list.

1. Are you mourning about anything in the past? If you have truly repented, confessed and made restitution where necessary, God has forgiven. Rejoice in that forgiveness from him, forgive yourself and resolve to be a 'Bethlehemite'.

2. Realise your need to be filled with the Spirit, so that he is free to teach you (Eph. 5:18).

3. Thank the Lord for what he is going to do as you become a meditator.

> Continual discoveries of what he has provided.
> He will show you what to do.
> You will not merely judge by outward appearance.
> The Holy Spirit will teach you.
> You will be able to worship him more and more.
> You will become strong in the Lord.
> You will be equipped for battle.
> You will have God given wisdom.
> You will be well balanced in truth.
> The Lord will be with you.
> You will be able to refresh others.

PRAYER

Father, I thank you for saving me, choosing me, and giving me your Holy Spirit to be my teacher. I desire to be skilful in your Word, strong in the Lord, equipped to do spiritual warfare in the name of the Lord Jesus. Thank you that you will give me your wisdom and enable me to be balanced in truth, with the evidence that you are with me, and please make me a refreshment to others. Amen.

And three of the thirty chief went down, and came to David in the harvest time unto the cave of Adullam: and the troop of the Philistines pitched in the valley of Rephaim.

And David was then in an hold, and the garrison of the Philistines was then in Bethlehem.

And David longed, and said, Oh that one would give me drink of the water of the well of Bethlehem, which is by the gate!

And the three mighty men brake through the host of the Philistines, and drew water out of the well of Bethlehem, that was by the gate, and took it, and brought it to David: nevertheless he would not drink thereof, but poured it out unto the Lord.

And he said, Be it far from me, O Lord, that I should do this: is not this the blood of the men that went in jeopardy of their lives? therefore he would not drink it (2 Sam. 23:13–17).

7 Meditation . . .

requirements for (3)

You cannot give what you do not have

Let us learn one more vital truth from Bethlehem about meditation. This incident was during the time when David was being hunted by King Saul. He was hiding in a cave called Adullam with his '3 D' men – discontented, distressed and in debt. The word 'Adullam' means 'a resting place', and although David may not have appreciated this meaning at that time, he was being prepared for kingship and learning to trust God in adverse circumstances. It is easy to rest in God when all circumstances are favourable and when there is no real pressure; but the real test of faith and our true ground of confidence is manifested when God either allows or ordains circumstances which are difficult. David is learning what he will later teach others:

> **Commit thy way unto the Lord; trust also in him; and he shall bring it to pass . . . Rest in the Lord, and wait patiently for him** (Ps. 37:5, 7).

One day, David came in from the heat of the sun and went to the water container for a drink. The water was warm and distasteful. Remembering the days of his youth, when hot and thirsty he could go to the well at Bethlehem and drink that cool, clear, refreshing liquid, he said, 'Oh, that one would give me drink of the water of Bethlehem, which is by the gate.' Three of his mighty men heard him express this desire and decided to give their king what he longed for. Bethlehem at this time was in the hands of the enemy. However, these three brave men broke through the enemy lines, drew the water from the well, fought their way back, and, tired and weary, returned to David carrying this precious treasure from Bethlehem.

David was deeply moved by the love, devotion and courage of these men as he received their gift from their hands. He realized this water had been obtained at the risk of their lives and would not drink it. We can imagine that touching scene as David goes out, probably in the early morning light, holding the water container, lifting his eyes to heaven and in an act of worship pours out every drop 'unto the Lord', saying, 'Be it far from me, O Lord, that I should do this. Is not this the blood of men that went in jeopardy of their lives? therefore he would not drink it.'

David's act of worship is a reminder to all who would meditate. We can only give to him what we receive from him, and when we receive living bread and living water from the house of bread, there is no other possible response. Why is the worship life of so many Christians so poverty stricken? One reason is they have drawn so little and therefore can give so little. The more the Word of God becomes part of our lives, the more of the Word we will pour out to the Lord. We have already seen that the knowledge of the glory of God, in the face of Jesus Christ, is treasure in earthen vessels; so the more knowledge we have of him, the more treasure we have; the more treasure we have, the more treasure we can present to him.

What happened when Abraham stood at the top of Mount Moriah? He presented God with the treasure that God had given him – Isaac. What happened to Hannah when she took young Samuel to the temple? She opened her treasure and gave to God what he had given to her. Through meditation there is the divine impartation of truth and revelation. God is the source of such gifts, and as we receive them, we have more to present to him.

Furthermore, we are encouraged to worship in the realisation that the Lord Jesus did not merely risk his life but gave his life. He broke down the wall of partition between us and God and made available the blessings of heaven. The Bethlehemite is ever mindful of the cost that has been paid to secure the blessings of the house of bread, and like a David, stand before God in awed worship and heartfelt thanks, having his life marked by the humility that becomes those who have received grace upon grace.

O come, let us adore him.

APPLICATION

Thank God for every trial and adverse circumstance in your life which has given you a thirst after God. As David went through this testing experience, and proved the faithfulness of God, so you can do the same.

There hath no temptation taken you but such as is common to man: but God is faithful, who will not suffer you to be tempted above that ye are able; but will with the temptation also make a way to escape, that ye may be able to bear it (1 Cor. 10:13).

PRAYER

Father, I thank you for every circumstance in my life which has given me a greater desire towards yourself. Thank you for your faithfulness, and for every lesson you have taught me and will teach me through the difficult times. Help me to feed on your Word, that I may have treasure to present to you in worship and in prayer. Thank you, Lord Jesus, for giving your life that I may be able to know you better day by day. Amen.

And he said unto them, Take heed what you hear: with what measure ye mete, it shall be measured to you: and unto you that hear shall more be given (Mark 4:24).

. . . The seed is the Word of God.

Those by the wayside are they that *hear*; then cometh the devil, and taketh away the word out of their hearts, lest they should believe and be saved.

They on the rock are they, which, when they *hear*, receive the word with joy; and these have no root, which for a while believe, and in time of temptation fall away.

And that which fell among thorns are they, which, when they have *heard*, go forth, and are chocked with cares and riches and pleasures of this life, and bring no fruit to perfection.

But that on the good ground are they, which in an honest and good heart, having *heard* the word, *keep* it, and bring forth fruit with patience (Luke 8:11–15).

8 Meditation . . .

companions of (1)

Hearing the Word

Having, I trust, settled in our hearts that the main priority of our lives is knowing God, and that one of the principle ways of acquiring this knowledge is through the Word of God, let us now consider the ways by which this knowledge can be received.

Hearing God's Word

Knowledge is impossible without communication, and God has chosen different means by which he makes himself known to us. One of these means is hearing the Bible being read. This happens, of course, every week, in every church, but how many times is Scripture read, a voice heard, and yet so little received? Jesus said to his disciples, 'having eyes, see ye not, and having ears, hear ye not' (Mark 8:18). To all the churches in Asia he says, 'he that hath an ear, let him hear what the Spirit saith unto the churches' (Rev. 2:7).

Hearing and listening

Because there is nothing more important that we will ever hear than the Word of God, it is worthy of our full attention. Two words are frequently used in Scripture: the word *hear*, and the word *hearken*. We can hear multitudes of words, and yet hear nothing apart from a sound, but when we *hearken* we give attention, we listen carefully, because we believe that what we are listening to is important. God has something to say to us in teaching, encouragement, correction, direction, exhortation, and we do not want to miss a thing. The promise of blessing is given to such an attentive listener in Proverbs:

> **Blessed is the man that heareth me, watching daily at my gates, waiting at the posts of my doors** (Prov. 8:34).

The prophet Amos predicted:

> **Behold, the days come, saith the Lord God, that I will send a famine in the land, not a famine of bread, nor a thirst for water, but of hearing the words of the Lord** (Amos 8:11).

He did not say there would be a famine of preaching, or conferences, or church services, or of books, but of hearing – properly listening to the Word of God.

Hearing and obeying

Continual obedience is necessary for continual hearing if the hearing is going to be effective. Moses made this clear:

> **And Moses called all Israel, and said unto them, *Hear*, O Israel, the statutes and judgments which I speak in your ears this day, that ye may *learn* them, and *keep*, and *do* them** (Deut. 5:1).

So it was expected when the people listened they would not only learn, but obey, and in the following chapter, verse 3, he promises they will be blessed by their obedience.

> ***Hear* therefore, O Israel, and observe to do it; that it may be well with thee, and that ye may increase mightily, as the Lord God of thy fathers has promised thee.**

We would do well to take the words of young Samuel: 'Speak, for your servant is listening.' James describes the folly of hearing without obedience:

> **But be ye doers of the word, and not hearers only, deceiving your own selves.**
> **For if any be a hearer of the word, and not a doer, he is like unto a man beholding his natural face in a glass:**

> For he beholdeth himself, and goeth his way, and
> straightway forgetteth what manner of man he was (Jas.
> 1:22–4).

Hearing and believing

Faith is essential in hearing God's Word, that is, we must believe what we are hearing. The writer to the Hebrews told them that the reason why so many Israelites failed to enter the promised land was because they did not believe the Word of God which they had heard.

> The word preached did not profit them, not being mixed
> with faith in them that heard it (Heb. 4:2).

Not only is faith necessary in hearing God's Word, but faith is increased by hearing.

> ... so then faith cometh by hearing, and hearing by the
> Word of God (Rom. 10:17).

Hearing and receiving

The hearing of obedience and faith will result in our receiving the truth, which will always lead us to an increased knowledge of God. In Proverbs 2:1–5 we have this confirmed:

> My son, if thou wilt receive my words, and hide my
> commandments with thee;
>   So that thou incline thine ear unto wisdom, and apply
> thine heart to understanding;
>   Yea, if thou criest after knowledge, and liftest up thy
> voice for understanding;
>   If thou seekest her as silver, and searchest for her as for
> hid treasures;
>   Then shalt thou understand the fear of the Lord, and find
> the knowledge of God.

Let me encourage you to listen to the Word of God. You can either buy Scripture tapes, or read the Word on to tapes yourself. Then when in the home, working, dressing, relaxing or travelling you can hear the Scriptures. Some years ago, a good friend of mine and I recorded the whole Bible on to tape. We got blessed reading it, and then blessed hearing it.

Let me encourage you in the future to give your full attention to the Word of God when it is read.

PRAYER

Father, I want to hear your voice and have ears to hear what you are saying to me through your Word. I desire my heart to be 'good ground' so that the seed planted there will bring forth fruit to your glory. Help me to know and recognise your voice so that I may follow you, my Good Shepherd. I choose to obey your Word, therefore be my teacher, and lead me in the way everlasting. Amen.

Seek ye out of the book of the Lord and read (Isa. 34:16).

Blessed is he that readeth, and they that hear the words of this prophecy, and keep those things which are written therein: for the time is at hand (Rev. 1:3).

Till I come, give attendance to reading, to exhortation, to doctrine (1 Tim. 4:13).

9 Meditation . . .

companions of (2)

Reading the Word

Paul wrote to Timothy, '. . . till I come, give attendance to reading.' One of the first things a new convert is told is to read the Bible. It is explained that when we receive the Lord Jesus into our lives we have a new friend. We cannot get to know our new friend unless he speaks to us, and we speak to him, and we speak about him. We speak to him in prayer, and he speaks to us in different ways, but one of the ways is by reading the Word of God.

The question if often asked, 'How should I read the Bible?' There are many suggested ways and systems which have been given and found to be beneficial. Most of these ways emphasise, and rightly so, the need for a definite plan and discipline to fulfil it. I would like to share a personal testimony.

Not long after I came into a personal relationship with Jesus Christ, I was having my 'quiet time' before going to business. The Lord spoke to me, telling me that I had never asked him how he wanted me to read through his book, and yet he had said to me 'In all thy ways acknowledge him, and he shall direct thy paths' (Prov. 3:6). I apologised to the Lord, and told him I had never really thought that was so important; as long as I read. I knew all the Bible was good, and did it matter where or how long I read it? I asked the Lord to show me his plan for me, and waited on him for a few minutes to receive the answer. He gave it to me by telling me to start at Genesis 1 and read a specific number of pages each day, and also to start at Matthew 1 and read the same number of pages. This I began to do, reading in both the Old and New Testament every day. I knew it was the Lord who gave me the number of pages to read, because I would not have chosen to read so much!

It was wonderful what happened after that. God spoke to me so many times, giving me teaching, warnings and instructions, not only in a general way, but related to my personal condition and circumstances. His call to me from business to full time ministry came through the normal reading of the Word. His direction regarding where to go and what his initial plans were for my wife and family came through the reading plan he had given to me.

I believe a very simple principle of God's guidance for those who have chosen to do the will of God is to keep doing what you are doing till he tells you to do something different.

A good plan for personal Bible reading will include:

(a) A definite reading programme.
(b) A time set aside to read, preferably at the beginning of the day or earliest opportunity. Some people say they are more alert at the end of the day than at the beginning. Professor Anderson, in his excellent book *The Quiet Time*, says, 'Why tune up the fiddle when the concert is finished?!'
(c) Prayer, asking God's help before you read.
(d) Marking your Bible, or making notes of specific things God says to you.

Here are some interesting facts about a normal reader:

(a) If you read the Bible 15 minutes each day, you would read through the whole Bible in less than a year.
(b) You could read the whole Bible in 71 hours, the Old Testament would take 52½ hours, the New Testament 18½.
(c) If you read by chapters, you could read the whole Bible in 18 weeks by reading 10 chapters a day.

Jesus said, 'If ye continue in my word, then are ye my disciples indeed; and ye shall know the truth, and the truth shall make you free' (John 8:31–2).

D. L. Moody, an American evangelist greatly used of God, gave testimony to the blessing of the reading of the Word in his own life. He said, 'I prayed for faith, and thought that someday faith would come down and strike me like lightning. But faith did not come. One day I read the tenth chapter of Romans, "Now faith cometh by hearing, and hearing by the Word of God." I had closed my Bible and prayed for faith. I now opened my Bible and began to *read* and my faith has been growing ever since.'

APPLICATION

1. Are you reading the Bible consistently, prayerfully, expectantly?
2. Are you disciplined in your reading?
3. Are you reading the way God wants you to read?

PRAYER

Father, I want to acknowledge you in all my ways. Forgive me, please, for every inconsistency in my life and lack of discipline which has robbed me of the knowledge of yourself. I choose to read your book the way you want me to. Please show me that way. Put your thoughts into my mind, as I wait upon you. I thank you that you promised that your sheep would hear your voice. I wait upon you in silence now, so that you may confirm to me whether to continue my present reading plan, or reveal any other way which you see is best for me. Amen.

Write down that plan here, and start *today*.

DATE:
This is my reading plan of the Bible:

Then shall we know, if we follow on to know the Lord: his going forth is prepared as the morning; and he shall come unto us as the rain, as the latter and former rain unto the earth (Hos. 6:3).

Teach me thy way, O Lord; I will walk in thy truth: unite my heart to fear thy name (Ps. 86:11).

10 *Meditation . . .*

companions of (3)

Studying the Word

Paul exhorted Timothy:

Study to show yourself approved unto God, a workman that needeth not to be ashamed, rightly dividing the word of truth (2 Tim. 2:15).

Studying the Word of God is a fascinating and rewarding devotional exercise. The word 'study' means to exert one's self; to endeavour, to give diligence. It is searching the Scriptures, collecting and collating facts on a theme, a doctrine, a character, a book, etc., in order to gain a greater knowledge of God. Paul commended the Bereans, 'these were more noble than those in Thessalonica, in that they received the Word with all readiness of mind, and *searched* the scriptures daily, whether those things are so' (Acts 17:11). The Bible is a gold mine with great treasure for those who will dig for it.

A. T. Pierson said of study, 'We should seek to find the total testimony of the inspired word upon each subject or theme, gathering up and arranging scattered or fragmentary hints, in an orderly and complete form. In the nature of the case, the Bible could not present a system of doctrine, yet it contains the material for such a system. It is the quarry rather than the structure; and it is for the student to bring together the material, discover its mutual relation, and construct out of it a full testimony of truth.'

Although Solomon said 'of making many books there is no end; and much study is a weariness of the flesh' (Eccles. 12:12), there is nothing boring or wearisome in studying something you love and in which you have a heart interest. For the maximum knowledge, we must use all the means available to acquire that knowledge. The glorious, continual discovery in studying the Word, is that the Word interprets the Word, proving over and over again the fact that it has one author.

Study requires both time and discipline, but the rewards are worth all the sacrifice and effort that is expended.

There are various helps for Bible study, such as:

1. *A good concordance.*
Young's Analytical Concordance is excellent, as is Strong's Exhaustive Concordance. With this concordance you can also obtain Thayers Greek-English lexicon which is numerically coded to the concordance, and also Gesenius' Hebrew-Chaldee lexicon to the Old Testament. These lexicons give detailed meaning of words which is a useful help.

2. *A good dictionary* such as Websters or the Oxford Dictionary.
It is important that we fully understand the meaning of the words we are using or studying.

3. *A good Bible dictionary or handbook.*
These give interesting insights into historical backgrounds of various books of the Bible, prevailing customs and other helpful data. Edersheim's *The Life and Times of Jesus Christ* gives much information of conditions during the life of the Lord here on earth.

4. *Other translations.*
Some translations are written more in the modern idiom, and give a clearer understanding of the meaning of some words. It must be understood, however, that there is a difference between a translation and a paraphrase. In most translations there has been a real attempt to adhere as closely as possible to the original text. A paraphrase is not always as correct as a translation, as the writer seeks to

put into his own words what *he* believes is the meaning of the original text.

5. *Note books.*
Preferably loose leaf, to enable you to add to your notes as more knowledge is acquired.

When studying a subject or theme, the writer recommends that you write down all the scriptures relating to it.

Draw two margins on your sheet. The purpose of the left hand margin being to write down the main point of the verse; and in the right margin the Scripture reference. For example, if you were making a study of what the Bible taught about itself, you could do it this way.

MAIN POINT	VERSE	REFERENCE
The book	Then said I, Lo, I come; in the volume of the book it is written of me.	Ps. 40:7
The book of the Lord	Seek ye out of the book of the Lord and read.	Isa. 34:16
The book of the law	This book of the law shall not depart out of thy mouth; but thou shalt meditate therein day and night.	Josh. 1:8
The book of the covenant	And the king went up into the house of the Lord, and all the men of Udah, and all the inhabitants of Jerusalem with him, and the priests, and the prophets, and all the people, both small and great: and he read in their ears all the words of the book of the covenant which was found in the house of the Lord.	2 Kgs. 23:2
The Word	But be ye doers of the Word, and not hearers only, deceiving your own selves.	Ja. 1:22
The Word of God	So then faith cometh by hearing, and hearing by the Word of God	Rom. 10:17

MAIN POINT	VERSE	REFERENCE
The Word of Christ	Let the Word of Christ dwell in you richly in all wisdom; teaching and admonishing one another in psalms and hymns and spiritual songs, singing with grace in your hearts to the Lord	Col. 3:16
The Word of life	Holding forth the Word of life; that I may rejoice in the day of Christ, that I have not run in vain, neither laboured in vain.	Phil. 2:16
The Word of truth	Of his own will begat he us with the word of truth, that we should be a kind of firstfruits of his creatures.	Ja. 1:18
The scriptures	Search the scriptures; for in them ye think ye have eternal life: and they are they which testify of me.	John 5:39
The sword of the Spirit	And take the helmet of salvation, and the sword of the Spirit, which is the word of God	Eph. 6:17

Having written out the verses, and put down the main point in the left hand margin, you get an over all view of the subject. When studying a theme, try to write down *all* the verses. Wrong interpretation of truth is sometimes caused by taking some verses and not all verses.

APPLICATION

If you do not have the 'tools' for study, plan to get them, either right away or over a period of time as you can afford them. Sometimes you can get good second-hand concordances, etc., at reasonable prices. Get equipped.

PRAYER

Father, thank you for all the riches and wealth there is in the Bible, and I do want to be a good student. Help me so to study that I may be approved unto God. Please help me never to forget that the purpose of study is to know you better, and not merely to amass knowledge for the sake of knowledge. Please help me to be trustworthy with the deposits of truth you will give me, and help me in everything to give you the glory.

Teach me thy way, O Lord. I will walk in thy truth. Unite my heart to fear thy name. This I ask in the name of the Lord Jesus. Amen.

Thy word have I hid in my heart, that I might not sin against thee (Ps. 119:11).

Remember the word which Moses the servant of the Lord commanded you (Josh. 1:13).

This second epistle, beloved, I now write unto you; in both which I stir up your pure minds by way of remembrance:
That ye may be mindful of the words which were spoken before by the holy prophets, and of the commandment of us the apostles of the Lord and Saviour (2 Pet. 3:1–2).

Sing unto the Lord, O ye saints of his, and give thanks at the remembrance of his holiness (Ps. 30:4).

. . . he shall *write* him a copy of this law in a book (Deut. 17:18).

Sing unto him, sing psalms unto him: *talk* ye of all his wondrous works (Ps. 105:2).

11 *Meditation . . .*

companions of (4)

Memorising; Singing; Writing; Speaking the Word of God

Memorising the Word

A friend, who was arrested in an East European country and later released, shared her resolve to memorise more scriptures. While in prison, with no Bible and now dependent only on her memory, she sought to recall verses from which she could obtain strength and comfort, but soon realised that the mental storehouse was not well stocked. Not one of us knows what lies ahead for the Church of God before the trumpet sounds, or what situations we will be in as individuals, in which we will need 'the comfort of the Scriptures' and be reliant on our memories. It is true that the Lord said of the Holy Spirit:

> **But the Comforter, which is the Holy Ghost, whom the Father will send in my name, he shall teach you all things, and bring to your remembrance, whatsoever I have said unto you** (John 14:26).

However, he can only bring to our remembrance what we have heard, read or memorised. It is not only in times of trouble that we need to know scriptures, but a memory well filled with the Word is necessary for our own personal edification and in sharing with others.

The children of Israel were continually exhorted to 'remember'.

> **Remember all the commandments of the Lord** (Num. 15:39).

67

Thou shalt remember all the way which the Lord led thee these forty years (Deut. 8:2).

Remember the words which Moses the servant of the Lord commanded you (Josh. 1:13).

Solomon wrote:

My son, forget not my law; but let thine heart keep my commandments (Prov. 3:1).

When the women came to the sepulchre and found the stone rolled away, and were perplexed and afraid, the two men in shining garments said to them,

. . . Why seek ye the living among the dead?
He is not here, but is risen: *remember* how he spake unto you when he was yet in Galilee (Luke 24:5–6).

Many people claim to have bad memories, but in most cases it is not really a bad memory but an untrained memory which is the problem. If you are in that category, why not give yourself a pleasant surprise. Select a verse, look at it, and read it aloud ten times, also quoting the Scripture reference at the beginning and at the end. Then close the Bible and repeat the verse. In most cases you will almost be word perfect. That great work, 'The Navigators', founded by Dawson Trotman, has been such a blessing to so many by encouraging people to memorise and apply scriptures.

The meditator is going to memorise many scriptures, even without deliberately doing so. As we shall see in a later chapter, as you ponder a verse word by word, and allow the Holy Spirit to apply it to your life, that word is going to be imprinted in your mind as well as your heart.

Singing the Word

Another means of learning the Word is by singing it. Most of the psalms are songs; and it is wonderful in these days that much worship in churches includes singing the Word of God. After all, there is nothing better we can give to God in worship that that which he himself inspired. We also memorise much of the Word by learning these scriptural songs.

A very good worshipful exercise is to sing some of the psalms in your personal devotions, putting your own music to the words. David encourages us:

> **Sing unto the Lord, O ye saints of his, and give thanks at the remembrance of his holiness** (Ps. 30:4).

> **Sing unto him a new song; play skilfully with a loud noise** (Ps. 33:3).

Paul wrote to the Ephesians:

> **. . . be filled with the Spirit;**
> **Speaking to yourselves in psalms and hymns and spiritual songs, singing and making melody in your heart to the Lord** (Eph. 5:18–19).

Writing God's Word

Frequently I have been amazed at what I have learned while writing out scriptures in times of study or message preparation. Details which have been missed in reading the verses are often noticed when you write them down. God, through Moses, gave clear instructions for future kings who would sit on the throne of Israel:

> **And it shall be, when he sitteth upon the throne of his kingdom, that he shall write him a copy of this law in a book out of that which is before the priests the Levites:**
> **And it shall be with him, and he shall read therein all the days of his life: that he may learn to fear the Lord his God, to keep all the words of this law and these statutes, to do them** (Deut. 17:18–19).

God knew how the Word could be impressed on their hearts by personally writing the law, and then continually reading it.

Speaking God's Word

Another way of learning the Word of God is through sharing with others. What blessing and exhilaration there is in conversing about the Lord and what he has said. Malachi reminds us that such conversations are recorded in heaven:

> **Then they that feared the Lord spake often one to another: and the Lord hearkened, and heard it, and a book of remembrance was written before him for them that feared the Lord, and that thought upon his name** (Mal. 3:16).

How hearts are warmed, and mutual edification experienced, when we share the bread of life with one another, as happened to the two on the way to Emmaus who walked and talked with Jesus and said, 'Did not our heart burn within us, while he talked with us by the way, and while he opened to us the scriptures?' (Luke 24:32).

Talking about the Word was also included in that comprehensive statement in Deuteronomy 6:4–9:

> *Hear*, O Israel: the Lord our God is one Lord:
> And thou shalt love the Lord thy God with all thine heart, and with all thy soul, and with all thy might.
> And these words, which I command thee this day, shall be in thine heart:
> And thou shalt *teach* them diligently unto thy children, and shalt *talk* of them when thou sittest in thine house, and when thou walkest by the way, and when thou liest down, and when thou risest up.
> And thou shalt bind them for a sign upon thine hand, and they shall be as frontlets between thine eyes.
> And thou shalt *write* them upon the posts of thy house, and on thy gates.

The more we become meditators, the more we will have to talk about and share with others.

APPLICATION

1. If you had no access to a Bible, how much of Scripture could you quote? Let the answer be a stimulus to encourage you to memorise.

2. Why not take a psalm now, and sing it to the Lord. For

example, take Psalm 100, sing it to the Lord, and use your own melody.

3. Having sung it, now write it out and note what you learned which you missed by reading.

Psalm 100

1.

2.

3.

4.

5.

4. Talk to someone today about what you learned, and share the Word.

PRAYER

Father, thank you for your Word, and for the various means by which I can get to know you through it. Please help me, as I apply myself to memorise your Word, and enable me to hide it in my heart. Accept my worship as I sing your Word, and teach me more, as from time to time I write it. Then, dear Lord, from an overflowing heart I desire to share your Word with others. Thank you, you will help me. Amen.

Part 2
MEDITATION

Verily, verily, I say unto you, he that believeth on me hath everlasting life.

I am that bread of life.

Your fathers did eat manna in the wilderness, and are dead.

This is the bread which cometh down from heaven, that a man may eat thereof, and not die.

I am the living bread which came down from heaven: if any man eat of this bread, he shall live for ever: and the bread that I will give is my flesh, which I will give for the life of the world (John 6:47–51).

12 *Meditation . . .*

definition of

As we now go into a study in depth on the subject of biblical meditation, let us again be reminded that a single strand of truth must be interwoven with other truth. Although meditation is probably the most productive of all the means of getting to know God through the Word, it is still only one of the means. It would not be right for anyone to say, 'Now I have found the answer, it is meditation.' It is not; it is a vital part of the answer, but as we have seen in previous chapters, it is also very important to hear, read, study, memorise, write, sing and speak the Word of God. So we come to the question, what is meditation? It is:

1. The inner reception of truth

Meditation is the devotional practice of pondering the words of a verse, or verses of Scripture, with a receptive heart, allowing the Holy Spirit to take the written Word and apply it as the living Word to the inner being. The result is the impartation of divine truth, being a response to God. Someone has described meditation as 'the digestive faculty of the soul'. Jeremiah wrote:

> **Thy words were found, and I did *eat* them; and thy word was unto me the joy and rejoicing of mine heart: for I am called by thy name, O Lord God of hosts** (Jer. 15:16).

Meditation is inwardly receiving the Word of God, illustrated by eating or feeding. God spoke to Ezekiel and emphasised this truth:

> **But thou, son of man, *hear* what I say unto thee; Be not**

thou rebellious like that rebellious house: open thy mouth, and *eat* that I give thee.

And when I looked, behold, an hand was sent unto me; and lo, a roll of a book was therein.

And he spread it out before me; and it was written within and without: and there was written therein lamentations, and mourning, and woe.

Moreover he said unto me, Son of man, *eat* that thou findest; *eat* this roll, and go speak unto the house of Israel.

So I opened my mouth, and he caused me to eat that roll.

And he said unto me, Son of man, cause thy belly to eat, and fill thy bowels with this roll that I give thee. Then did I eat it, and it was in my mouth as honey for sweetness (Ezek. 2:8–10; 3:1–3).

More truth . . . more life

The Lord Jesus made this wonderful statement in John 6:63:

It is the spirit that quickeneth; the flesh profiteth nothing: the words that I speak unto you, they are spirit, and they are life.

Therefore, the more of the Word we inwardly receive, the more life we receive. This is one of the basic ways for spiritual growth. His words are living words; they are 'spirit and life' words, and as they are imparted to us, our spiritual capacity is increased. In the temptation in the wilderness, the Lord rebuked the devil, who had said 'If thou be the Son of God, command that these stones be made bread,' by quoting from the Old Testament and saying, 'It is written, Man shall not live by bread alone, but by every word that proceedeth out of the mouth of God' (Matt. 4:3–4). God's words have *life*.

As it is so important to understand this vital truth, let us look at another scripture. Peter is teaching the importance of the knowledge of God, and says this of God's Word:

Whereby are given unto us exceeding great and precious promises: that by these ye might be partakers of the divine

nature, having escaped the corruption that is in the world through lust (2 Pet. 1:4).

In other words, Peter is saying that when you believe a promise of God, you receive something of God himself, something of his divine nature. Let me illustrate. Supposing you came to faith in Jesus Christ in a church service. The Spirit of God convicted you of your sin, and you heard the great news that God loves you and that Jesus died for you. Now somewhere there came to you 'an exceeding great and precious promise'. It may have been the promise of John 3:36:

He that believeth on the Son hath everlasting life.

What happened when this word was believed and inwardly received? You were given everlasting life. Now, everlasting life is something of the divine nature. You received something of God himself. There is a promise I like to take to the Lord every morning, because every morning I am a candidate:

If any of you lack wisdom, let him ask of God, that giveth to all men liberally, and upbraideth not; and it shall be given him (Jas. 1:5).

When I admit to God that my human wisdom is insufficient to do the will of God, to make the right decisions, to cope with the varied circumstances of every day living, and ask him for wisdom, believing and receiving his promise, he gives me some of *his* wisdom. Now wisdom is part of the divine nature, so the more I receive, the more I grow, and the more I grow, the more of his life will be manifested through me. Through meditation there is a continual impartation of his word, his truth and his life.

More truth . . . more light

Not only is there life in truth, but there is also light. The psalmist said:

The entrance of thy words giveth light; it giveth understanding to the simple (Ps. 119:130).

Notice David says it is the 'entrance' of the Word that gives light. Not merely looking at truth, or admiring truth, or agreeing with truth – but inwardly receiving it. In Exodus 16 we read of God's provision of manna to the children of Israel. Here was 'bread from heaven' to feed and sustain them. What did the people do when they saw it – admire it, analyse it, dissect it? No. They ate it, inwardly received it. This is what happens in true meditation, and as we receive more truth, more of the Word, we also receive more light. Jesus said, 'Ye are the light of the world' (Matt. 5:14), and we will shine brighter and brighter as we allow his Word to enter our hearts, and that same Word will illuminate our way and be 'a lamp unto my feet, and a light unto my path' (Ps. 119:105).

2. Revelation

Meditation is receiving revelation through the Word. Truth which vitally affects our lives, and changes them, does not come merely by explanation, but by revelation. Most of us can remember truths we have read or heard ministered, and we knew they must be true because they were in the Bible, but there was no heart understanding. Then one day we said, 'Now I see it!' What happened? Did we have a sudden increase in our I.Q.? No, we received revelation, and that truth became meaningful and part of our life.

Many times a verse, or verses of Scripture, are like flowers which have closed their petals because the sun has gone down. You look at the flower, and admire it because it is part of God's creative miracle, but there is much beauty you cannot see. In the morning, when the sun rises, the flower begins to open up towards the light, and then you can see the full beauty and colours and details. In the same way, we can look at Scripture and know it is good because God is the author, and yet fail to behold the beauty and detail it contains. However, while you meditate, dependent on divine illumination by the Sun of righteousness, there comes revelation and insight, giving you increased knowledge of the Creator, and an impartation of knowledge of which you now become a steward. This reminds us how dependent we are on the Holy Spirit to give us such revelation. Paul reminds us of this in 1 Corinthians 2:9–12

> ... it is written, Eye hath not seen, nor ear heard, neither have entered into the heart of man, the things which God hath prepared for them that love him.
> *But God hath revealed them unto us by his Spirit*: for the Spirit searcheth all things, yea, the deep things of God.
> For what man knoweth the things of man, save the spirit of man which is in him? even so the things of God knoweth no man, but the Spirit of God.
> Now we have received, not the spirit of the world, but the Spirit which is of God; that we might know the things that are freely given to us of God.

We have received the Spirit that we might know. Always remember in meditation that you are completely dependent on the Holy Spirit to give you such revelation. Do not lean to your own understanding or intellectual abilities. The right attitude for receiving revelation is illustrated in an incident in the life of Solomon. Soon after coming to the throne, the Lord revealed himself to the king in a dream and said, 'Ask what I shall give thee.' His response to this great offer was:

> ... O Lord my God, thou hast made thy servant king instead of David my father: and I am but a little child: I know not how to go out or come in ...
> Give therefore thy servant an understanding heart to judge thy people, that I may discern between good and bad: for who is able to judge this thy so great a people? (1 Kgs. 3:7,9).

Let us emulate Solomon's example, so that we, too, might receive revelation.

1. *He was obedient.*
Revelation is dependent on obedience. In verse 3 of the same chapter it says, 'Solomon loved the Lord, walking in his statutes.' Not only is revelation dependent on obedience, but continual revelation is dependent on continual

obedience. The stopping place in the lives of many Christians has been that place of failure to obey revealed truth, and that person can stay there for years, without any spiritual progress, or increase in the knowledge of God. 'Then shall we know, if we follow on to know the Lord' (Hos. 6:3). 'If ye continue in my word, then are ye my disciples indeed' (John 8:31).

2. *He was a servant.*

He came to God to get the orders, not to give them. The servant-heart attitude is essential for revelation.

> **Behold, as the eyes of servants look unto the hand of their masters . . . so our eyes wait upon the Lord our God** (Ps. 123:2).

We are servants: we are called upon to minister to the Lord and minister to others. We discover through his word his instructions, and the servant obeys. And yet there is an ever increasing realm of intimacy for those who will obey him, as Jesus said to his disciples:

> **Ye are my friends, if ye do whatsoever I command you.**
> **Henceforth I call you not servants; for the servant knoweth not what his lord doeth: but I have called you friends; for all things that I have heard of my Father I have made known unto you** (John 15:14–15).

3. *He was childlike.*

'I am but a little child' said Solomon to God. And so for revelation we need to be childlike (not childish). We need the humility of a child, the sense of dependence of a child, the confident trust of a child, the openness of a child. Jesus called a little child to him one day, and said to those he taught:

> **Except ye be converted, and become as little children, ye shall not enter into the kingdom of heaven.**
> **Whosoever therefore shall humble himself as this little child, the same is the greatest in the kingdom of heaven** (Matt. 18:3–4).

Humility acknowledges the need of revelation, and the dependence on another to give that revelation.

4. *He was a king.*
Although coming as a servant, and as a child, he recognised and acknowledged the position that God had given him. 'Thou hast made thy servant king.' So it is with us, as we come to God for the unveiling of himself and of his truth. We, too, recognise the grace of God in making us sons of the living God, joint heirs with Jesus Christ, children of God, and children of the King. We have been brought into relationship and fellowship, and he delights to speak to us, to teach us, to comfort us, to warn us, to build us up, because we have become inseparably linked with himself. He delights to manifest himself to those who obey him, as Jesus said:

He that hath my commandments, and keepeth them, he it is that loveth me: and he that loveth me shall be loved of my Father, and I will love him, and will *manifest myself* to him (John 14:21).

Summary

Meditation is the practice of pondering, considering, and reflecting on verses of Scripture in total dependence on the Holy Spirit to give revelation of truth and meaning, and by obedient response and reception of that Word, having it imparted to the inner being. The impartation of such truth brings life and light to the meditator, as a result of coming with the attitude of humility, trust and obedience.

Meditation is inwardly receiving truth. It is feeding on Christ, living Bread and living Word. The word, *meditate*, is taken from the Latin root word, *medicalus*, from which we get our word, medicine; and medicine, we know, never does any good in the bottle, it has to be taken internally, normally three times a day!

APPLICATION

1. Write down your understanding of the meaning of meditation.

2. What are the essential attitudes necessary for receiving revelation?

PRAYER

Father, I thank you that by your grace and mercy I am a son of God, and a child of the King. I thank you that you delight to reveal yourself to me through your Word. I come to you now like a little child, depending on you completely to give me revelation which I desire and choose to obey. Let your Word indeed be a lamp unto my feet, and a light unto my path. Amen.

Let the redeemed of the Lord say so, whom he hath redeemed from the hand of the enemy (Ps. 107:2).

O how love I thy law! it is my meditation all the day (Ps. 119:97).

I rejoice at thy word, as one that findeth great spoil (Ps. 119:162).

13 *Meditation . . .*

blessings of

'What is the secret of your success?' is the question which is often asked of those who have prospered. The answer normally gives some vital principles which have been applied and certain keys which have been used. It is both interesting and instructive to discover the reasons why men and women have been spiritually prosperous, and left an imprint for the kingdom of God, in glorifying him and blessing others. One of the essential ingredients for such prosperity is meditation on the Word of God. Let us look at some of these, so that we may be encouraged to be meditators.

David

It is most interesting how the wonderful book of Psalms begins. In the very first chapter we are given one of the main reasons why David had such a capacity for God, skill in worship, depth of knowledge of God, and an understanding of the ways of God – he had learned to meditate. He did not have much of the written Word; he never went to a Bible or theological college; but he did meditate on the Word he had, and meditated on God and the works of God. Meditation to David was not merely a duty or formality, it was the very joy of his heart, causing him to cry 'O how love I thy law! it is my meditation all the day (Ps. 119:97). Meditation gave him an ever increasing knowledge of God, and love for God, and he is described as 'the man who was raised up on high, the anointed of the God of Jacob, and the sweet psalmist of Israel' . . . 'David, Who found favour before God' . . . 'a man after mine own heart, which shall fulfil all my will' . . . 'thy servant David', etc. (2 Sam. 23:1; Acts 7:46; 13:22; 4:25). He was a successful shepherd, soldier, song writer and sovereign, and was living evidence of what he wrote in Psalm 1 of the meditator, 'Whatsoever he doeth shall prosper.'

Joshua

Joshua was given the great responsibility of leading the children of Israel into the promised land. He had taken on this monumental task of leadership from Moses, the man of God. Before him was a country occupied by enemies, walled cities and even giants. Such a task was going to require courage, wisdom and skill.

At the very commencement of his leadership, God spoke to him, and placed, as it were, in his hands one of the vital keys for his life, to enable him to lead the people in victory. It was meditation. God said,

> . . . be thou strong and very courageous, that thou mayest observe to do according to all the law, which Moses my servant commanded thee: turn not from it to the right hand or to the left, that thou mayest prosper whithersoever thou goest.
> This book of the law shall not depart out of thy mouth; but thou shalt *meditate* therein day and night, that thou mayest observe to do according to all that is written therein: for then thou shalt make thy way prosperous, and then thou shalt have good success (Josh. 1:7–8).

He did obey God, and he did have good success, and led the people to victory.

The testimony of George Muller

In the early 1830s George Muller, challenged by the faithlessness of so many of his contemporaries, longed to have something to point to, in his words, 'as visible proof' that God our Father is the same faithful God as ever he was; as willing as ever to prove himself to be the living God, faithful to all who would trust him and live according to his divine principles. God gave him the desire of his heart by leading him to initiate a project for the housing and care of orphans in the city of Bristol, England. George Muller looked to God for every provision, not looking to man, but to God, and the history of the George Muller homes is a vibrant testimony to the faithfulness of God. His life, ministry and work was an inspiration and blessing to thousands.

He testified to the great value of biblical meditation in his own life by a written testimony entitled *Soul Food*, in which he states:

> It has pleased the Lord to teach me a truth, the benefit of which I have not lost for fourteen years. I saw more clearly than ever that the first business to which I ought to attend every day, was to have my soul happy in the Lord. The first thing to be concerned about, was not how much I might serve the Lord, but how I might get my soul in a happy state, and how my inner man might be nourished. I might seek truth to set it before the unconverted, I might seek to benefit believers, I might seek to relieve the distressed, and I might in other ways seek to behave myself as it becomes a child of God in this world, and yet, not being happy in the Lord, and not being strengthened in the inner man day by day, all this might not be attended to in the right spirit.

> Before this time my practice had been to give myself to prayer after having dressed in the morning. Now I saw the most important thing I had to do was to give myself to the reading of the Word of God, and to *meditate* on it, thus my heart might be comforted, encouraged, warned, reproved, instructed, and that thus, by means of the Word of God, my heart might be brought into experimental communion with the Lord.

> I began therefore to *meditate* on the New Testament from the beginning, early in the morning. The first thing I did after having asked in a few words the Lord's blessing upon his Word, was to begin to meditate on

the Word, searching, as it were, every verse to get a blessing out of it . . . not for the sake of public ministry, not preaching, but for obtaining food for my soul.

The result I found to be invariably this. After a few minutes my soul had been led to confession, or thanksgiving, or intercession, or supplication, yet it turned almost immediately to prayer. When thus I have been for a while making confession, or intercession, or supplication or having given thanks, I go to the next words of the verse, turning all as I go into prayer for myself or others, as the Word may lead to it, but still continually keeping before me that food for my own soul is the object of my meditation.

The difference, then, between my present practice and my former is this. Formerly, when I arose, I began to pray as soon as possible, and generally spent all my time till breakfast in prayer, or almost all the time. At all events I almost invariably began with prayer, except when I felt my soul to be more than usually barren, in which case I would read the Word. But what was the result? I often spent a quarter of an hour, or half an hour, or even an hour on my knees before having been conscious to myself of having derived comfort, encouragement, humbling of the soul, etc., and often after having suffered much from wandering thoughts, for up to half an hour, I only then began to really pray.

I scarcely ever suffer in this way now, for my heart being brought into experimental fellowship with God, I speak to my Father about the things he has brought to me in his precious Word.

It often astonishes me that I did not sooner see this point.

George Muller proved that biblical meditation was a life changing devotional practice.

A Bible College president

Reverend Jim Argue, the president of a continually growing Bible College, writes:

God has blessed Genesis Discipleship School with continued numerical growth, that has necessitated four new buildings in the first six years of operation.

I believe a major contributing factor is our priority emphasis on a student's life, or state of being, rather than their ministry and much doing. I know of no single emphasis in our curriculum that produces a vibrant, vertical love relationship with God more than biblical meditation.

How fortunate we were that God sent Campbell McAlpine our way to share this truth when the foundation of our school's study programme was being laid.

A housewife

Here are excerpts from a letter from Mrs Betty Rawlins, of Salem, Oregon, who, after being a Christian for thirty-five years, has had her life revolutionised by the Lord through his Word.

. . . I was faithful to my church in attendance and Christian works, but inside I felt empty because I knew I did not have an intimate relationship with God. Quite by accident (or so I thought at the time), my husband and I sat under the teaching of Campbell McAlpine on Bible Meditation. The facts he presented, I knew immediately, were the solution to my seeking God, and becoming acquainted with him. He gave practical steps, and I made a covenant with God concerning meditation on his Word each day.

Today, after years of longing and searching, words just cannot express what is happening in my heart and life as a result of obedience and discipline in spending time daily in meditating in God's Word, and allowing the Holy Spirit to reveal to my heart the very heart of God. Some days I am aware of his greatness and awesomeness; other days I receive promises of his blessings for me and my family. Even his discipline is sweet because I know he loves me and desires an intimate walk with me. Each day I come with eager anticipation to wait on God and the revelation of himself through his Word, and to praise him – some mornings I feel as if I will burst from the fulness of his presence.

For fifteen years I had been oppressed with fears of all kinds – unreasonable, and unfounded – but very real to me. Now my heart has never been so full of praise to God, who knows me so intimately, and speaks to each need of my heart.

A business man

I recently received a letter from a business man in San Antonio, Texas. Eddie Eskew is manager of a large chain store. This is what he wrote:

This month is the third anniversary in meditating on the Word of God. I felt I must tell you some of the wonderful things that have happened as results of meditating. After the first month I realised I did not need any medication for my ulcer, or any more tranquilliser pills. Six months after I began meditating, I entered into a very bad business situation. Rather than worrying, I turned it over to the Lord and stayed in his Word. I never lost any sleep or had any negative thoughts. Praise God, I was healed of worry and fear.

Through God's Word, I have been able to have more discipline in my life. My eating, sleeping, and working habits are completely changed. Now I get up at 6 a.m., meditate until 7, then go jogging for three and a half miles before breakfast.

One morning a few weeks ago, as I was jogging God told me that he had renewed my youth. I feel better physically and spiritually than I have in twenty-five years.

I have also learned how to meditate night and day. The last thing I do at night is meditate on one or two verses, letting them be my last conscious thought. I go to sleep immediately. When I awake, the Word of God is my first thought. Praise God for your teaching on meditation.

Your testimony

If you will make meditation an integral part of your life, you, too, will have a testimony, even after a few months. For this reason space is left underneath, so that you may record the transformation and blessing that has come to your life.

My personal testimony to the blessing of meditation

I commenced to meditate on (date)

Blessed is the man that walketh not in the counsel of the ungodly, nor standeth in the way of sinners, nor sitteth in the seat of the scornful.

But his delight is in the law of the Lord; and in his law doth he meditate day and night.

And he shall be like a tree planted by the rivers of water, that bringeth forth fruit in his season; his leaf also shall not wither; and whatsoever he doeth shall prosper.

The ungodly are not so: but are like the chaff which the wind driveth away.

Therefore the ungodly shall not stand in the judgment, nor sinners in the congregation of the righteous.

For the Lord knoweth the way of the righteous: but the way of the ungodly shall perish (Ps. 1:1–6).

14 *Meditation . . .*

promises of (1)

The testimonies in the previous chapter are evidence of the fulfillment of some of the promises God gives to the meditator. We are now going to consider these 'exceeding great and precious promises', which are great encouragements. Whenever promises are given in Scripture, it is wise to look for two things: firstly, what God says he will do, and secondly, what God tells us to do. If the conditions are fulfilled, then the promise also will be fulfilled. Here they are, as we find them in Psalm 1.

1. HAPPINESS

'Blessed is the man . . . that doth meditate,' is the initial promise. The word 'blessed' here means 'O happy man' or 'O the happiness of man'. Our loving God and Father not only wants us to be happy, but tells us how we can be happy through meditation and application of the Word of God. Other scriptures confirm this, such as:

. . . Blessed is the man that feareth the Lord, that delighteth greatly in his commandments (Ps. 112:1).

Blessed are the undefiled in the way, who walk in the law of the Lord (Ps. 119:1).

Blessed are they that keep his testimonies, and that seek him with the whole heart (Ps. 119:2).

He that keepeth the law, happy is he (Prov. 29:18).

Blessed is he that readeth, and they that hear the words of this prophecy, and keep those things which are written therein: for the time is at hand (Rev. 1:3).

Do you want to be happy? . . . Then meditate.

2. FRUITFULNESS

He shall be like a tree planted by the rivers of water,
that bringeth forth his fruit in his season.

**Not only does God promise happiness to the meditator,
but he also promises fruitfulness. This should be the
desire of every child of God, because fruitlessness is
a tragedy. Fruit is the evidence of right relationship
and fellowship with God. It distinguishes between the
false and the true. The Lord said:**

**Beware of false prophets, which come to you in sheep's
clothing, but inwardly they are ravening wolves.**

**Ye shall know them by their fruits. Do men gather grapes
of thorns, or figs of thistles?**

**Even so every good tree bringeth forth good fruit; but a
corrupt tree bringeth forth evil fruit.**

**A good tree cannot bring forth evil fruit, neither can a
corrupt tree bring forth good fruit.**

**Every tree that bringeth not forth good fruit is hewn
down, and cast into the fire.**

Wherefore by their fruits ye shall know them (Matt. 7:15–
20).

One morning Jesus and his disciples left the town of
Bethany. 'Bethany' means 'the house of figs', and Jesus felt
hungry. On the outskirts of the town he noticed a fig tree
in the distance, and walked towards it, so that his hunger
could be satisfied. Mark records the story:

**And seeing a fig tree afar off having leaves, he came, if
haply he might find any thing thereon: and when he came
to it, he found nothing but leaves; for the time of figs was
not yet.**

**And Jesus answered and said unto it, No man eat fruit of
thee hereafter for ever** (Mark 11:13–14).

From a distance the tree looked attractive, and promis-
ing, but it could not stand close inspection. Leaves, the

94

outward appearance, may impress men, but the Master was looking for fruit to satisfy him. Because the tree could not meet his need, it could not meet the need of others. The same Lord comes to our lives, not to be impressed by outward appearance, or cloak of piety and religion, but fruit, which is the manifestation of his own life within us.

Unfruitfulness brings judgment

John the Baptist preached,

> **And now also the axe is laid unto the root of the trees: therefore every tree which bringeth not forth good fruit is hewn down, and cast into the fire** (Matt. 3:10).

and the Lord Jesus said,

> **Every branch in me that beareth not fruit he taketh away** (John 15:2).

Unfruitfulness brings disappointment to the Lord

He has given us so much, and made everything available so that we might give him pleasure. How disappointed he must be when he fails to find fruit from our lives. Something of this disappointment is expressed in the parable he told in Luke 13:6–9. A man had a vineyard, and in it he planted a fig tree. For three years he came to the tree hoping to find fruit, but each year he was disappointed – there was nothing. He told his servant to cut the tree down, but the servant asked him to give it another chance – another year – and if it didn't produce within that year, then it could be cut down. Is your life producing fruit? Meditation is one of the means necessary for fruit production. Is the Lord giving you another chance?

Unfruitfulness is a failure to use what has been given

Again, to emphasise the importance of fruitfulness, the Lord told the parable in Luke 19:12–26, of a man, who, before going on a long journey, called his ten servants giving each of them a pound, and telling them to 'occupy till I come'. When he returned he called each to give account of how they had used what he had given. One said his investment had produced 1,000 per cent; another 500 and they were well rewarded by their master for their diligence. However, another came and said,

> ... here is thy pound, which I have kept laid up in a napkin.
> For I feared thee, because thou art an austere man: thou takest up that thou layest not down, and reapest that thou didst not sow (Luke 19:21).

There was no reward for this man. He was an unfaithful steward with what he had been given, and he had a completely wrong assessment of his master's character. He abundantly rewarded the faithful servants, but the unfaithful servant forfeited the reward, even losing that which he had been given.

One of the greatest things the Lord has given us is his Word. Let's use it.

What is fruit?

Fruit is the result of the outworking of the life of the Lord Jesus in us. We cannot produce it, he can. Read and reread John 15. Jesus said in his discourse on the vine and the branches, 'As the branch cannot bear fruit of itself, except it abide in the vine; no more can ye, except ye abide in me' (v. 4). The life that flows through the branch is the life of the vine, producing the fruit of the vine; so with us, it is 'not I, but Christ'. He is the vine, we are the branches, and as we yield our lives to his control, and walk in obedience and total dependence on him, fruit will be the result. We are indwelt by his very life, by the Spirit who produces the fruit described thus:

> For the fruit of the Spirit is in all
> > Goodness
> > Righteousness
> > Truth (Eph. 6:9).

But the fruit of the Spirit is
  Love
  Joy
  Peace
  Longsuffering
  Gentleness
  Goodness
  Faith
  Meekness
  Temperance   (Gal. 5:22–3).

Fruit is the product of divine wisdom.

But the wisdom that is from above is first
  Pure
  Peaceable
  Gentle
  Easy to be entreated
  Full of mercy
  Good fruits
  Without partiality
  Without hypocrisy   (Jas. 3:17).

But now being made free from sin, and become servants to God, ye have your fruit unto
  Holiness   (Rom. 6:22).

The fruit of the righteous is a tree of life; and he that
  Winneth souls
is wise   (Prov. 11:30).

By him therefore let us offer the
  Sacrifice of praise to God continually,
that is, the fruit of our lips
  Giving thanks to his name   (Heb. 13:15).

The importance of fruitfulness

As we understand the importance of fruitfulness, we will be diligent in the application of its requirements

1. *It is one of the purposes of being chosen by Christ.*

Ye have not chosen me, but I have chosen you, and ordained you, that ye should go and bring forth fruit, and

97

that your fruit should remain: that whatsoever ye shall ask of the Father in my name, he may give it you (John 15:16).

2. *It is the evidence of a right relationship with God.*

Wherefore, my brethren, ye also are become dead to the law by the body of Christ, that ye should be married to another, even to him who is raised from the dead, that we should bring forth fruit unto God (Rom. 7:4).

3. *It is the proof of pleasing God.*

That ye might walk worthy of God unto all pleasing, being fruitful in every good work and increasing in the knowledge of God (Col. 1:10).

The requirements of fruitfulness

Here again we must blend truth with truth. Meditation is an essential ingredient for fruitfulness because without the Word of God we will be barren. Here are the requirements:

1. *Abiding in Christ.*

Abide in me, and I in you. As the branch cannot bear fruit of itself unless it abide in the vine; no more can ye, except ye abide in me (John 15:4).

'Abide' simply means 'remain'. When you received the Lord Jesus, God forgave your sins and placed you in Christ. In order that his life may flow through you, you have to remain where you have been placed. You remain in Christ the same way you were placed in him – by faith.

Faith is hearing God's Word and acting upon it. That is how you abide. You hear his Word that you are a branch, and you believe it. Faith acknowledges our position in Christ, that his life is in us.

2. *The Word of God.*

But his (the meditator's) delight is in the law of the Lord, and in his law doth he meditate day and night. And he shall

**be like a tree planted by the rivers of water, that bringeth
forth his fruit in his season** (Ps. 1:2–3).

**If ye abide in me and my words abide in you, ye shall ask
what ye will and it shall be done unto you** (John 15:7).

**But he that received seed into the good ground is he that
heareth the word, and understandeth it; which also beareth
fruit, and bringeth forth, some an hundredfold, some sixty,
some thirty** (Matt. 13:23).

3. *Death to one's own life and desires*

**Verily, verily, I say unto you, Except a corn of wheat fall
into the ground and die, it abideth alone: but if it die, it
bringeth forth much fruit** (John 12:24).

We have already seen that we cannot of ourselves bring
forth fruit. In order that his life can produce that fruit, it
is obvious that we must die to our self-effort, self-confidence,
self-reliance, self-ambition, self-glory, self-righteousness,
because self cannot produce spiritual life. '. . . he that soweth to his flesh shall of the flesh reap corruption; but he
that soweth to the Spirit shall of the Spirit reap life everlasting (Gal. 6:8).

4. *Chastening and pruning.*

Because we are God's children through faith in Christ, he
loves us as a Father, supplies our needs as a Father, and
corrects us as a Father.

**Now no chastening for the present seemeth to be joyous,
but grievous: nevertheless afterward it yieldeth the
peaceable fruit of righteousness unto them which are
exercised thereby** (Heb. 12:11).

Correction, cleansing and purging are essential not merely for producing fruit, but for producing more fruit. Again
referring to John 15, we read in verse 2:

**Every branch that beareth fruit, he purgeth, that it may
bring forth more fruit.**

Many times in meditation, God takes the Word as his

correcting and purging instrument, revealing sometimes wrong attitudes, wrong motives or wrong desires, and as the Holy Spirit takes that Word and convicts us, as we respond, we are cleansed and purged.

5. *Trusting and hoping in God.*
Jeremiah gives the same truth as David in the first psalm, encouraging us to trust and hope in God, that we might be fruitbearers.

> **Blessed is the man that trusteth in the Lord, and whose hope the Lord is.**
> **For he shall be as a tree planted by the waters, and that spreadeth out her roots by the river, and shall not see when heat cometh, but her leaf shall be green, and shall not be careful in the year of the drought, neither shall cease from yielding fruit** (Jer. 17:7–8).

6. *The power of the Holy Spirit.*
Fruit bearing is evidenced by our influence on others, both by witness of the life and witness by the word. The power for such witness is the power of the Holy Spirit.

> **But ye shall receive power after that the Holy Ghost is come upon you; and ye shall be witnesses unto me** (Acts 1:8).

How refreshing is the story of the Acts of the apostles – what power, what influence, what fruit! Ordinary people filled with extraordinary power, made available to them and to every child of God. When we come with our open, yielded lives to our blessed Lord Jesus, who said

> **. . . If any man thirst, let him come unto me and drink.**
> **He that believeth on me, as the scripture hath said, out of his belly shall flow rivers of living water.**
> **(But this he spake of the Spirit which they that believe on him should receive: for the Holy Ghost was not yet given; because that Jesus was not yet glorified)** (John 7:37–9).

then we, too, can know that fullness, and go on 'being filled with the Spirit' (Eph. 5:18). . . . Thirst . . . come to me . . .

100

drink ... believe on me ... out of shall flow ... Do not be numbered among those who have not because they ask not ... ask and ye shall receive that your joy may be full.

7. *Rooted and grounded in Christ Jesus.*
As we 'abide in him' and let the Word of God dwell in us richly, dead to ourselves, receiving his correction and pruning, trusting and hoping in God, filled with the Spirit, we will be rooted and grounded in Christ Jesus, to be fruitful for his glory.

> **As ye have therefore received Christ Jesus the Lord so walk ye in him.**
> **Rooted and built up in him, and stablished in the faith, as ye have been taught, abounding therein with thanksgiving** (Col. 2:6–7).
>
> **And the remnant that is escaped of the house of Judah shall again take root downward, and bear fruit upward** (Isa. 37:31).

Meditation enables the roots to go downwards in the depths of the knowledge of God, and from that deposit of divinity will come forth fruit that will remain.

APPLICATION

1. *Fruit inspection*
Let us now apply some of the truths of this chapter by asking and replying to these questions:

(a) What does the Lord find in my life – leaves only, or fruit?
(b) Am I living to impress others or please God?
(c) Am I 'abiding in him' in total dependence on his life to produce fruit?
(d) Have I died to my self, to be alive unto God?

2. *Tell the Lord what you want to be*

PRAYER

Father, thank you so much that you chose me to bring forth fruit. I acknowledge that of myself I cannot do this, but I praise you that I am in Christ, and he is in me. I yield myself totally to you, trusting you to enable me as I walk in obedience to let your life flow through me. Fill me with your Holy Spirit, as I surrender to the Lordship of Jesus. I am so looking forward to getting to know you better through meditating on your Word, so that being rooted and grounded in you, I will not disappoint you, or be a bad steward of all you have given, but continually give you pleasure and joy. Amen.

15 *Meditation . . .*

promises of (2)

We are continuing in this chapter to consider the promises God gives to those who meditate. These promises are divine guarantees to all who fulfil the conditions. To the promises of happiness and fruitfulness, we now add the promise of:

3. FRESHNESS

. . . he shall be like a tree planted by the rivers of water, that bringeth forth his fruit in his season; *his leaf also shall not wither*; and whatsoever he doeth shall prosper (Ps. 1:3).

The meditator will never wither. According to Webster's dictionary, to wither means to cause to fade and become dry; to decay; to become sapless, and lose vigour. I remember, when speaking at a conference in New Zealand, meeting a man who was over eighty years of age. He was over six feet tall, with a freshness and joy that made it difficult to believe he had reached the four score mark. He gripped my hand and said, 'Praise the Lord, my brother.' I thought at the time how wonderful it was to meet an elderly saint who had never withered. It is also good to meet a middle aged Christian who has never withered, or even a young Christian who has not withered!

What a glorious prospect for the meditator. Through all the seasons of life, he or she will be evergreen, because of being 'planted by the rivers of water', abiding in Christ, and feeding on the Word of God. When a new convert includes meditation as a daily practice, he will not fade in the 'spring' of his Christian life. When 'summer' comes, with all the heat of circumstances, he will not fade. In the 'autumn' or 'fall', when the leaves of others are fading and falling, still there will be that freshness in his life. When 'winter' comes he will know the fulfillment of Psalm 92:12–14:

> **The righteous shall flourish like the palm tree: he shall grow like a cedar in Lebanon.**
> **These that be planted in the house of the Lord shall flourish in the courts of our God.**
> **They shall still bring forth fruit in old age; they shall be fat and flourishing.**

Scripture gives reasons why people do wither. When we know the causes, then we know what to avoid.

1. *Failure to receive the Word of God.*
When the Lord was giving his discourse on the parable of the sower and the seed, he likened the seed to the Word of God, and the ground to the heart. Describing the shallow reception of the Word he said:

> **Some fell upon stony places, where they had not much earth, and forthwith they sprung up, because they had no deepness of earth:**
> **And when the sun was up, they were scorched; and because they had no root, they withered away** (Matt. 13:5–6).

2. *Failure to abide in Christ.*

> **If a man abide not in me, he is cast forth as a branch, and is withered; and men gather them, and cast them into the fire, and they are burned** (John 15:6).

3. *Forsaking the Lord.*
When Isaiah the prophet was calling to an apostate nation to return to God, he warned:

> **. . . they that forsake the Lord shall be consumed . . . For ye shall be as an oak whose leaf fadeth, and as a garden that hath no water** (Isa. 1:28,30).

Withered lives have withered joy. Joel, describing those who were in this state, wrote 'all the trees of the field, are withered; because joy is withered away from the sons of men' (Joel 1:12).

How different is the experience of the meditator. He is like a tree planted by rivers of water. He is continually refreshed by new revelations of the wonder and glory of God, and can say with David, 'O how love I thy law! it is my meditation all the day. . . I rejoice at thy word, as one that findeth great spoil' (Ps. 119:97,163).

What encouragement, what incentive to meditate. Receive the promises as your own, the promise of happiness, fruitfulness, and freshness – and still there is more!

4. PROSPERITY

Whatsoever he doeth shall prosper.

This must be one of the greatest promises in the Bible for a Christian. Imagine a business consultant approaching the principals of a large corporation and offering them a particular system, which, if adopted, would absolutely guarantee profit and success. Man's systems can fail, but God's guarantees are certain.

When you become a meditator you can personalise this promise and say, 'Whatsoever I do will prosper.' Although our loving heavenly Father has promised to meet all our needs, and may give us material wealth, the main prosperity offered is spiritual prosperity. A Christian can have much wealth but be a pauper in the knowledge of God, while some who have little of this world's goods are spiritual millionaires, because of their wealth of the riches of the knowledge of God and intimate fellowship with him. I remember being in Marseilles, in the south of France, and walking through one of the poor districts of that great city with a friend. We found the address we were looking for, and climbed up several flights of stairs to a small attic apartment. In this room, sparsely furnished, there lived a delightful Russian couple, who loved the Lord. The joy of the Lord overflowed from them and they sang to us in Russian that wonderful hymn, 'How great thou art'. What a sanctuary that room was, how rich were the occupants. It is not the court that makes the palace, but the presence of the King.

Again let us intertwine truth, bringing together the conditions of spiritual prosperity. Each of these is included in the practice of biblical meditation:

1. *Seeking the Lord.*
Seeking the Lord means setting our hearts with faith and diligence, to wait on him, to inquire of him in prayer and in the Word, that we might know him, and his will. Seeking God brings spiritual prosperity. This was proved by a godly king of Judah called Hezekiah. He had succeeded his wicked father, Ahaz, and under his leadership there was a time of spiritual restoration. He called the people back to God and obedience to his will. He was a man that sought God, and this is given as one of the reasons for his prosperity. It is written of him:

And thus did Hezekiah throughout all Judah, and wrought that which was good and right and truth before the Lord his God.
   And in every work that he began in the service of the house of God, and in the law, and in the commandments, *to seek his God*, he did it with all his heart, and *prospered*.
(2 Chron. 31:20–1).

His prosperity was associated with the Word of God, 'the law and the commandments', into which he inquired to know the will of God. Another king, Uzziah, discovered the secret of success. It is recorded of him, 'as long as he sought the Lord, God made him to prosper' (2 Chron. 26:5).

The seeking heart is necessary in meditation: 'beyond the sacred page we seek thee, Lord' . . . 'but the true seeker always finds' . . . 'he that cometh to God must believe that he is, and that he is a rewarder of them that diligently seek him (Heb. 11:6). Solomon records some of these rewards.

I love them that love me; and those that seek me early shall find me.

Riches and honour are with me; yea, durable riches and righteousness.

My fruit is better than gold, yea, than fine gold; and my revenue than choice silver.

I lead in the way of righteousness, in the midst of the paths of judgment:

That I may cause those that love me to inherit substance; and I will fill their treasures (Prov. 8:17–21).

2. *Obeying the Lord.*

The second condition for prosperity is obedience. Before Solomon became king of Israel, David his father gave him this wise counsel:

Now, my son, the Lord be with thee; and *prosper* thou, and build the house of the Lord thy God, as he hath said of thee.

Only the Lord give thee wisdom and understanding, and give thee charge concerning Israel, that thou mayest keep the law of the Lord thy God (1 Chron. 22:11–12).

3. *Believing the Lord.*

The third condition for prosperity is believing God and his Word. When God delivered Daniel from the power of the lions, it is written:

. . . So Daniel was taken up out of the den, and no manner of hurt was found upon him, because he *believed in his God.*

So this Daniel *prospered* in the reign of Darius, and in the reign of Cyrus the Persian (Dan. 6:23,28).

Jehoshaphat, king of Judah, encouraged his people as they faced an enemy which greatly outnumbered them, with these words:

. . . *Believe* in the Lord your God, so shall ye be established; believe his prophets, so shall ye *prosper* (2 Chron. 20:20).

4. *Living in the consciousness of his presence.*

God desires us to live in the consciousness of his presence, and the knowledge that he is with us. Through Christ we have been brought into living relationship with him, to have continual access to himself, the living God. What grace, what mercy, what privilege!

Therefore being justified by faith, we have peace with God through our Lord Jesus Christ.

By whom also we have access by faith into this grace wherein we stand and rejoice in the hope of the glory of God (Rom. 5:1–2).

His presence with us makes us prosperous. When Joseph was a slave in Potiphar's house in Egypt, we read:

And the *Lord was with Joseph*, and he was a *prosperous* man; and he was in the house of his master the Egyptian.

And his master saw that the Lord was with him, and that the Lord made all that he did to *prosper* in his hand (Gen. 39:2–3).

5. *Meditating in the Word of God.*

Prosperity is promised to all who will meditate continually in the Word of God. Meditation includes all the essentials for prosperity: seeking the Lord; obeying the Lord; trusting the Lord; knowing the presence of God with us. When Joshua took over the leadership of the children of Israel, God gave him the key for success.

This book of the law shall not depart out of thy mouth; but thou shalt meditate therein day and night, that thou mayest observe to do according to all that is written therein: for then thou shalt make thy way *prosperous*, and then thou shalt have *good success* (Josh. 1:8).

Bring all these things in to harmony in your life, and you, too, will be successful. Solomon wrote, 'buy the truth, and sell it not' (Prov. 23:23), that is, give all that is necessary to obtain truth, but give nothing to lose it.

110

APPLICATION

1. Thank the Lord for the prospect of a happy, fruitful, unfading, and prosperous life, as you decide to meditate continually in God's Word.

2. Ask the Lord to help you, and teach you to
   Seek the Lord
   Obey the Lord
   Believe the Lord
   Live with the consciousness of his presence

PRAYER

Father, I thank you for access to yourself through the Lord Jesus. I believe that I am in him and he is in me, and that I can live by faith knowing that you are with me.

Save me, please, from withering, but help me as I seek you, obey you, trust you and meditate in your Word, to be like a tree that bringeth forth its fruit in its season, causing me to prosper for your glory. Amen.

Blessed is the man that walketh not in the counsel of the ungodly, nor standeth in the way of sinners, nor sitteth in the seat of the scornful.

But his delight is in the law of the Lord; and in his law doth he meditate day and night (Ps. 1:1–2).

16 *Meditation . . .*

conditions of (1)

Having reviewed the wonderful promises given to the meditator, let us now look at the conditions which are necessary for their fulfillment.

Separation from sin

The first condition is non-alliance with the ungodly, the sinner, and the scornful.

> **Blessed is the man that walketh not in the counsel of the ungodly, nor standeth in the way of sinners, nor sitteth in the seat of the scornful.**

Paul voices the same sentiments:

> **Be ye not unequally yoked together with unbelievers: for what fellowship hath righteousness with unrighteousness? and what communion hath light with darkness?**
>
> **And what concord hath Christ with Belial? or what part hath he that believeth with an infidel?**
>
> **And what agreement hath the temple of God with idols? for ye are the temple of the living God; as God hath said, I will dwell in them, and walk in them; and I will be their God, and they shall be my people.**
>
> **Wherefore come out from among them, and be ye separate, saith the Lord, and touch not the unclean thing; and I will receive you,**
>
> **And will be a Father unto you, and ye shall be my sons and daughters, saith the Lord Almighty** (2 Cor. 6:14–18).

Although we are called to separation, we are not called to isolation. Jesus was a friend of sinners. We can have sinner friends without being involved in their sins, but desiring to influence them for God and be sign posts to the Lord Jesus. This kind of friendship excludes being emotionally involved, or having close friendships with those who, as yet, do not know the saving grace of our Lord Jesus Christ. If we walk in the counsel of the ungodly, and stand with them in their ways, we will soon be sitting with them. When praying for his disciples, the Lord said of them:

> . . . they are not of the world, even as I am not of the world. I pray not that thou shouldest take them out of the world, but that thou shouldest keep them from the evil.
> They are not of the world, even as I am not of the world.
> Sanctify them through thy truth: thy word is truth (John 17:14–17).

There will never be a depth of understanding of the Word of God when there is a divided heart, with love for the world. John pleads with the early church,

> Love not the world, neither the things that are in the world. If any man love the world, the love of the Father is not in him.
> For all that is in the world, the lust of the flesh, and the lust of the eyes, and the pride of life, is not of the Father, but is of the world.
> And the world passeth away, and the lust thereof: but he that doeth the will of God abideth for ever (1 John 2:15–17).

The true meditator will be separated from the world. The Word either separates people from the world, or the world separates people from the Word. Such separation does not restrict true happiness, but enhances it. The devil's suggestion to our first parents in Eden was that if they obeyed God they would be the losers, and he is still whispering the same lie today. But God says, 'blessed is the man' – very happy is the man – who is separated. It is good to understand what is meant by 'the world'. It is not merely something which is external – gambling, immorality, drunkenness, etc. Spiritual warfare is not only against worldly ways, but against the spirit of the world. The world is unregenerate human nature, whenever or wherever it is found, either in the church or outside the church. Whether the world is manifested in distasteful outward form, or in subtle and refined ways, we must recognise it and repudiate it. James emphatically writes:

Ye adulterers and adulteresses, know ye not that the friendship of the world is emnity with God? whosoever therefore will be a friend of the world is the enemy of God (Jas. 4:4).

Choose to be separated from sin, and separated unto God. Choose to love God and not the world. Embrace the cross of our Lord Jesus, and stand with the apostle Paul in total agreement as he declares:

But God forbid that I should glory, save in the cross of our Lord Jesus Christ, by whom the world is crucified unto me, and I unto the world (Gal. 6:14).

When you make this resolve there will be revelation of truth by 'the spirit of truth, whom the world cannot receive', bringing you into an ever increasing likeness to him who was 'holy, harmless, undefiled, separate from sinners' (Heb. 7:26).

Thank God, not only for the saving work of the cross, but also for it's separating work. Here is an excerpt from an article written by that twentieth century prophet, the late Dr A. W. Tozer, entitled 'The Old Cross and the New':

The old cross would have no truce with the world. For Adam's proud flesh it meant the end of the journey. It carried into effect the sentence imposed by the law of Sinai. The new cross is not opposed to the human race, rather it is a friendly pal, and if understood aright, it is the source of oceans of good clean fun, and innocent enjoyment. It lets Adam love without interference.

His life motivation is unchanged, he still lives for his own pleasure, only now he takes delight in singing choruses and watching religious films, instead of singing bawdy songs, and drinking hard liquor. The accent is still on enjoyment, though the fun is now on a higher plane morally, if not intellectually.

The new cross encourages a new and entirely

different evangelistic approach. The evangelist does not demand abnegation of the old life before the new life can be received. He seeks to key into public interest, by showing that Christianity makes no unpleasant demands, rather it offers the same thing the world does, only on a higher level. The new cross does not slay the sinner, rather it redirects him. The old cross is a symbol of death. It stands for the abrupt and violent end of a human being. The man in Roman times who took up his cross and started down the road had already said farewell to his friends. He was not coming back. He was not going out to have his life redirected. He was going to have it ended. The cross made no compromise, modified nothing, it slew all of the man, completely and for good. It struck cruel and hard, and when it had finished its work the man was no more.

The race of Adam is under death sentence. There is no communitation, and no escape . . . our message is not a compromise, but an ultimatum.

What are the results of such separation? They are so many – friendship with God; true happiness; fruitfulness; spiritual prosperity; and God says, 'I will be a Father unto you, and ye shall be my sons and daughters, saith the Lord Almighty.'
Are you a candidate?

PRAYER

Father, I want to glory in the cross of the Lord Jesus, and acknowledge it separates me from the world. I choose to be separated from the world. Please give me a continual love for those who do not know you, and let my life and witness speak of you. I do not want to walk in the counsel of the ungodly, or stand in the way of sinners, or sit in the seat of the scornful, and I thank you, you are able to keep me from evil and evil influence. I want to know the fear of God which is to hate evil, keeping me free from love for the world. Please reveal yourself to me through your Word, and let it

have such an abiding place in my life, that I will be clean
through the words you speak unto me, as Jesus promised.
Amen.

But his delight is in the law of the Lord; and in his law doth he meditate day and night (Ps. 1:2).

I delight to do thy will, O my God: yea, thy law is within my heart (Ps. 40:8).

Delight thyself also in the Lord; and he shall give thee the desires of thine heart (Ps. 37:4).

17 Meditation . . .

conditions of (2)

The second essential the psalmist gives to the meditator is to delight in the law, or teachings, of the Lord. To delight simply means to take pleasure. This will be an increasing experience in the life of the meditator, as new discoveries are made in the Word of the wonders of God and his ways. David is speaking out of the depths of his own experience, and there is the unmistakable evidence in his writings that God's Word gave him absolute joy. Several of these pleasurable outbursts are found in Psalm 119:

And I will delight myself in thy commandments, which I have loved (v. 47).

Thy testimonies also are my delight and my counsellors (v. 24).

The law of thy mouth is better unto me than thousands of gold and silver (v. 72).

How sweet are thy words unto my taste! yea, sweeter than honey to my mouth! (v. 103)

Thy word is very pure: therefore thy servant loveth it (v. 140).

I rejoice at thy word, as one that findeth great spoil (v. 162).

David certainly did not find God's Word dry, dull or boring! Why? We can find two main reasons which we will now consider.

DELIGHTING IN THE LORD

One cannot delight in the Word without delighting in the author. As it was with David, so it should be with us. He loved God – God was his pleasure, his joy, his life. He determined it would be so, and it was. He said, 'I *will* love thee, O Lord' (Ps. 18:1), and because he sought to please God, he could also say, 'I love the Lord' (Ps. 116:1). One of the principal ways of showing our love for God, and our delight in him, is to inquire, and discover and fulfil the things that give him pleasure. In other words, what delights him will delight us. Here are some of these things:

1. *Loving those who love God.*

> **I love them that love me; and those that seek me early shall find me** (Prov. 8:17).

As God gets great pleasure from those that love him, so we, too, should find joy and pleasure in their company and fellowship.

2. *Obeying God.*
Jesus said, 'He that hath my commandments, and keepeth them, he it is that loveth me: and he that loveth me shall be loved of my Father, and I will love him, and will manifest myself to him' (John 14:21).

3. *Following after righteousness.*
Solomon wrote, 'The way of the wicked is an abomination unto the Lord: but he loveth him that followeth after righteousness' (Prov. 15:9).

When we do the thing that is right, and set our hearts to be upright in all our transactions and ways, it pleases the heart of God.

4. *Serving God in the right way.*
Paul wrote:

> **For the kingdom of God is not meat and drink; but righteousness, and peace, and joy in the Holy Ghost.**
> **For he that in these things serveth Christ is acceptable to God, and approved of men** (Rom. 14:17–18).

Joyless service gives him no pleasure. This was one of

God's complaints against Israel. . . 'thou servedst not the Lord thy God with joyfulness, and with gladness of heart, for the abundance of all things' (Deut. 28:47). However, when we minister to the Lord in the right way, with peace in our hearts towards God and men and gladness in our souls, God's wonderful heart is well pleased. Jesus the Son always served the Father this way, causing him to speak from heaven and say, 'This is my beloved Son, in whom I am well pleased' (Matt. 3:17; 17:5).

5. *Giving cheerfully to the Lord.*
Giving is like serving; both should be done with joy. In one of Paul's chapters on giving, he wrote to the Corinthians:

Every man according as he purposeth in his heart, so let him give; not grudgingly, or of necessity: for God loveth a cheerful giver (2 Cor. 9:7).

John McNeil, a Scottish minister, was once ministering on this text, and described a cheerful giver as a man in a church who shouted out, 'Hallelujah, here comes the collection plate.' Such joyous outbursts are rarely heard at offering time! How bountiful God is to us, and it gives him great joy to give. May we give great joy to him, and really believe 'it is more blessed to give, than to receive'.

6. *Praying with a heart that is right.*
How God loves to hear us, and what pleasure he receives when we pray with a sincere heart. 'The prayer of the upright is his delight' (Prov. 15:8). Not only praying right but also . . .

7. *Praising God with a heart that is right.*
Here is another reason why David composed and sang so many songs to God; he knew God enjoyed it. Because of this he determined to worship God. In Psalm 69:30–2 he writes:

I will praise the name of God with a song, and will magnify him with thanksgiving.
    This also shall *please the Lord* better than an ox or bullock that hath horns and hoofs.

The humble shall see this, and be glad: and your heart shall live that seek God.

What an incentive to praise the Lord; not only in church, but as often as we can. Meditation will produce much praise, and thanksgiving and worship.

8. *A broken and contrite heart.*
Multitudes have been blessed by the recorded humility, brokenness and confessions of David after his adultery with Bathsheba, and ordering the death of her husband, Uriah. God hates sin, but he is merciful to the truly repentant, who respond to the convicting work of the Holy Spirit. Like the prodigal's father, he welcomes and delights to see the wanderer come back to himself. David said,

For thou desiredst not sacrifice; else would I give it: thou delightest not in burnt offering.
The sacrifices of God are a broken spirit: a broken and a contrite heart, O God, thou wilt not despise (Ps. 51:16–17).

9. *Seeking to please God in everything.*
Giving pleasure to God can be summed up in the words of Paul to the church at Colosse:

For this cause we also, since the day we heard it, do not cease to pray for you, and to desire that ye might be filled with the knowledge of his will in all wisdom and spiritual understanding;
That ye might walk worthy of the Lord unto all pleasing, being fruitful in every good work, and increasing in the knowledge of God;
Strengthened with all might, according to his glorious power, unto all patience and longsuffering with joyfulness (Col. 1:9–11).

2. DELIGHTING IN THE WILL OF GOD

The natural sequence of delighting in the Lord will be delighting in his will. David said:

I delight to do thy will, O my God: yea, thy law is within my heart (Psalm 40:8).

The will of God is not meant to be a mere obligation, but a pleasure. The Word of God reveals what that will is, and when we receive that Word as David said 'within my heart', obedience will be a joy. How important it is to be convinced that the will of God is not just something which is good, but that which is the best. There is no lasting peace, or joy or fulfillment outside that will. Therefore, we should yield ourselves totally to God, that we might not only know his will, but do it. The surrender of ourselves to God is absolutely necessary for the knowledge of his will, as Paul exhorted the Christians in Rome:

I beseech you therefore, brethren, by the mercies of God, that ye present your bodies a living sacrifice, holy, acceptable unto God, which is your reasonable service.
And be not conformed to this world: but be ye transformed by the renewing of your mind, that ye may prove what is that good, and acceptable, and perfect, will of God (Rom. 12:1–2).

Choosing to do the will of God is essential for the meditator. The Lord Jesus said:

If any man will do his will, he shall know of the doctrine, whether it be of God (John 7:17).

Submission to God will cause a free flow of revelation through the Word, as we borrow the words of the Lord Jesus when he said, 'I seek not mine own will, but the will of the Father which hath sent me' (John 5:30).

DELIGHTING IN HIS WORD

When the Lord himself and his will is our delight, then our meditations of him shall be sweet. This pleasure will increase as we continue to hear his voice and contemplate him. Meditation is not a technical exercise, but a loving relationship, in which he communes with us and we commune with him. Let us take time now to apply some of these truths.

APPLICATION

Be still before the Lord now. Tell him you want to delight in him, in his will and in his Word. Ponder some of the things that please him, and make them applicable in your life:

Loving those who love God
Is there someone you do not love – some resentment, bitterness, something unforgiven? Confess it before the Lord, and pray God's blessing on that person or persons, so that from your heart the Holy Spirit can shed abroad the love of God. This will please him.

Obeying God
He has promised to manifest himself to us when we obey him. Choose to be obedient and thus give him joy.

Following after righteousness
Tell him you choose to do the right thing, being upright and honest in all your dealings with God and men, and serving him with the right motive to glorify him. Ask the Lord to help you serve him with joy, because you love him.

Giving
From today do not give grudgingly, or because it is the right thing to give the tithe to God, and then above that your offerings, but give cheerfully as an expression of love.

Praying and praising
How wonderful that today we can please him by our prayers and praises. How glorious that not only does he hear us, but he delights to hear us.

Delighting in his will

Yield yourself to him, by presenting your body. When he has your body, he has everything, because housed within your body is your soul and spirit. Now take the words of David as yours and say, 'I delight to do thy will, O my God . . .'

Delighting in his Word

Thank him in joyous anticipation that his Word is going to be your joy and pleasure, because it is his voice to you.

PRAYER

My Father, I come to you in the name of the Lord Jesus, realising without him I can do nothing. I want to give you pleasure and joy, delighting in you, and your will, and your Word. Here is my body which I present to you. It is not mine in any case, because it has been bought with the precious blood of your beloved Son, my Saviour, Jesus. I acknowledge that, and only give to you what rightfully belongs to you.

Please help me, by the power of the Holy Spirit, to love what you love, and hate what you hate. Save me, Lord, from a joyless service and powerless life. Help me to love all that you love, to be obedient to all that you tell me, to live uprightly, to give cheerfully, to pray and praise you with a pure heart, and not only to do your will, but to delight in it.

Thank you for all the revelation of yourself that I am going to receive through your Word. I do want to delight in that, too, so will you please help me? I want your Word to be the voice of my beloved to my heart, the comfort and guidance of my Good Shepherd, the loving instructions from my perfect teacher, light from you, *the* Light, and truth from you, *the* Truth.

You are so gloriously and majestically delightful, and I thank and praise and worship you. Amen.

And they drew nigh unto the village, whither they went: and he made as though he would have gone further.

But they constrained him, saying, Abide with us: for it is toward evening, and the day is far spent. And he went in to tarry with them.

And it came to pass, as he sat at meat with them, he took bread, and blessed it, and brake, and gave to them.

And their eyes were opened, and they knew him; and he vanished out of their sight . . .

And he said unto them, These are the words which I spake unto you, while I was yet with you, that all things must be fulfilled, which were written in the law of Moses, and in the prophets, and in the psalms, concerning me.

Then opened he their understanding, that they might understand the scriptures (Luke 24:28–31, 44–5).

18 *Meditation . . .*

its practice (1)

Having considered the conditions for the meditator, we now come to the practice of this rewarding devotional application of God's Word. The story of the Lord meeting with the two disciples on the Emmaus road, and his subsequent time in their home, illustrates certain truths which need to be applied in meditation.

1. SITTING WITH THE LORD

When the Lord accepted the invitation into the home, it is recorded that 'he sat at meat with them'. This is the first requirement for the meditator; to sit relaxed with the Lord. This obviously does not mean that we can only meditate in a sitting position, but indicates a rest and relaxation in the Lord as we open his Word. As we meet with him, he is there to meet with us. Meditation starts with a restful waiting on the Lord, allowing the Holy Spirit to bring our hearts and minds into focus on himself and his Word. We may have been busy with so many things, but now we come to meet with the Lord, putting aside distracting thoughts, so that we can hear his voice. As Wesley wrote:

> Expand thy wings, celestial dove,
> Brood o'er our natures night,
> On our disordered spirits move,
> And let there now be light.

Solomon said, 'I sat down under his shadow with great delight, and his fruit was sweet to my taste' (S. of S. 2:3). Before Jesus fed the 4,000, he commanded the people to sit down first. Ask the Lord to help you to come in to a place of rest in himself as you wait upon him. You can do various things to help you in this way, such as speaking to the Lord, reading some scriptures, singing a worshipful chorus or song, or sitting silently in his presence. This may take a minute, or a few minutes, but just as long as is required to bring you to that attitude of restful attention, to hear him speak through the Word. Never let your mind go blank, but think of him – there are too many things waiting for blank minds. I am not giving you a formula, but simple helps.

2. HEARING THE VOICE OF THE LORD

As meditation is hearing God speak to us through his Word, it is important to know and to recognise his voice. We could not sit comfortably with the Lord if there was any undealt with sin, or disobedience, which would interfere with fellowship with him. 'If I regard iniquity in my heart, the Lord will not hear me,' but in the next verse David can say, 'but verily the Lord hath heard me; he hath attended to the voice of my prayer' (Ps. 66:18,19), because his heart was right with God.

Impressions come from four main sources:

Other people
Ourselves
The devil
God

While meditating you are usually on your own, so are uninfluenced by other people. Because we want his thoughts and not our own, it is important to deal with our thoughts, as we prepare to hear from God. How can we do this?

Impressions from ourselves

Proverbs 3:5–6 tells us:

Trust in the Lord with all thine heart; and lean not unto thine own understanding.

In all thy ways acknowledge him, and he shall direct thy paths.

Bring this as a prayer to God, with a sincere heart, and tell Him you come trusting him to speak to you through the Word, and that you are not depending on your own understanding, or intellect, because 'he that trusteth in his own heart is a fool' (Prov. 28:26). Tell him that you acknowledge him in all your ways, and trust him to direct your paths; and thank him that you are going to hear his voice. We are totally dependent on him and his Holy Spirit to help us receive his thoughts. Isaiah 55:8–11 reminds us:

For my thoughts are not your thoughts, neither are your ways my ways, saith the Lord.

For as the heavens are higher than the earth, so are my ways higher than your ways, and my thoughts than your thoughts.

For as the rain cometh down, and the snow from heaven, and returneth not thither, but watereth the earth, and maketh it bring forth and bud, that it may give seed to the sower, the bread to the eater:

So shall my word be that goeth forth out of my mouth: it shall not return unto me void, but it shall accomplish that which I please, and it shall prosper in the thing whereto I send it.

What an encouraging scripture; assuring us that as we are open to his thoughts and to his ways, the Word of God will come to us, to do its work within us, to accomplish the purposes of God. How wonderful that we *can* bring our own thoughts into that place of subjection to his. Paul reminded us of this:

For though we walk in the flesh, we do not war after the flesh:

(For the weapons of our warfare are not carnal, but mighty through God to the pulling down of strongholds;)

Casting down imaginations, and every high thing that exalteth itself against the knowledge of God, and bringing into captivity every thought to the obedience of Christ (2 Cor. 10:3–5).

Impressions from the devil

We do have an enemy, but he has been defeated by our blessed Lord Jesus. However, we are not ignorant of his devices. He does not want Christians to be strong in God through the knowledge of God, but there is protection from any inroads he would seek to bring, and we can take our stand against him in the name of the Lord Jesus. Arm yourself with these scriptures, and use them with faith whenever you are conscious of his attacks or diversions, and also as your protection:

Submit yourselves therefore to God. Resist the devil, and he will flee from you (Jas. 4:7).

Ye are of God, little children, and have overcome them: because greater is he that is in you, than he that is in the world (1 John 4:4).

And they overcame him by the blood of the Lamb, and by the word of their testimony; and they loved not their lives unto the death (Rev. 12:11).

***Humble* yourselves therefore under the mighty hand of God, that he may exalt you in due time:**
Casting all your care upon him; for he careth for you.
Be sober, be vigilant; because your adversary the devil, as a roaring lion, walketh about, seeking whom he may devour:
Whom *resist* stedfast in the faith, knowing that the same afflictions are accomplished in your brethren that are in the world (1 Pet. 5:6–9).

Put on the whole armour of God, that ye may be able to stand against the wiles of the devil . . .
Stand therefore, having
Your loins girt about with *truth*.
Having on the breastplate of *righteousness*
Your feet shod with the preparation of the *gospel of peace*
Above all, taking the shield of *Faith*
Take the helmet of *salvation*,

And the sword of the Spirit, which is the *Word of God*.

Praying **always with all prayer and supplication in the Spirit, and** *watching* **thereunto with all perseverance, and supplication for all saints** (Eph. 6:11, 14–18).

When we come against the enemy, submitted to God, and in the name of the Lord Jesus, resisting him, then he must flee, and we will therefore not receive any impressions from him. Praise God for his victory, and in him we can be continual overcomers.

Impressions from God

Having dealt with the other sources of impression, we now trust the Lord to speak to us through the Word, and know that he will. All that he says will glorify his name, causing us to worship him. It will agree with the rest of his Word, and will impart knowledge of himself. It will not cause us to be 'puffed up' with knowledge, but will enable us to love him more, and others more. What he says will be 'true, honest, just, pure, lovely, and of good report'. It will be the voice of the Good Shepherd which we, his sheep, will recognise, and follow. His Word will be 'the joy and rejoicing' of our heart, because we have come to him saying, 'Speak Lord, for thy servant heareth', knowing that we will never be disappointed. We will go from our times of meditation with a sense of awe and wonder because we have heard the voice of the Almighty. His word will linger and return because it has been imparted to us, becoming part of the very fibre of our being, bringing life, and light, and the knowledge of the Holy.

3. RECEIVING MEAT

We read that 'Jesus sat at meat with them.' Meditation will give us the meat of the Word. When we start in our Christian life, we start with 'milk',

> **As newborn babes, desire the sincere milk of the word, that ye may grow thereby** (1 Pet. 2:2),

but it is tragic when a Christian continues on milk. This was the complaint of Paul in writing to the Corinthians:

And I, brethren, could not speak unto you as unto spiritual, but as unto carnal, even as unto babes in Christ.

I have fed you with milk, and not with meat: for hitherto ye were not able to bear it, neither yet now are ye able.

For ye are yet carnal: for whereas there is among you envying, and strife, and divisions, are ye not carnal, and walk as men? (1 Cor. 3:1–3).

A missionary, who had been much used of God in China, was once asked how he read the Bible. He replied, 'I take plenty of potatoes every day, and a little meat.' When asked to explain his remark, he said, 'I read many pages of the Bible every day – that is like potatoes, it is filling; but I meditate on one or two verses every day – that is the meat, that is the nourishment:' and that is a very good balanced diet! After Jesus had fed the 5,000, and the crowds continued to follow him, no doubt hoping for another similar miracle, he said to them:

Labour not for the meat which perisheth, but for that meat which endureth unto everlasting life, which the Son of man shall give unto you: for him hath God the Father sealed (John 6:27).

Look forward to receiving much meat as you become a meditator.

Christ the giver

The Emmaus story confirms we are completely dependent on the Lord to feed us from and with his Word. As the disciples sat at the table with Jesus, *he* took the bread, *he* blessed it, *he* brake it, *he* gave it to them. They sat and received it. So it is in meditation; we read a verse (or verses), we ponder it, consider it, contemplate it; but *he* is the one who gives revelation and understanding. Meditation is not an intellectual exercise, although God does not bypass our minds. It is not a puzzling of what the Scripture means; nor is it a delving into some commentary to get another's thoughts (good as they may be), but it is allowing the Master to impart to us from his own loving hand.

The result was, 'their eyes were opened, and they knew him.' They received not merely a revelation of truth, but a revelation of Christ. Although he disappeared out of their sight, the wonder and joy remained, and with burning hearts they rushed into Jerusalem to share with their fellow Christians what they had received from the Master. This leads us into a very vital truth about meditation which we will consider in another chapter, but let it be underlined in our hearts – *meditation always brings a response*. Would you please verbalise that statement, because it is so important – meditation always brings a response.

APPLICATION

Consider the various points of this chapter and then make them matters for prayer:

Sitting with the Lord.
    Some find this easier than others because of their temperaments. Some may have a placid disposition, and others a restless one, but both need the help of the Lord. Share with the Lord any difficulties you have in this realm, and tell him what specific help you need. Why not write them down:

Hearing God's voice.

Have you had difficulty in detecting what has been your voice, his voice, or the voice of the enemy? Tell the Lord about it, and tell him you want to hear his voice more clearly. Apply the teaching of this chapter, looking to him and not leaning to your own understanding.

Take God's protection against the enemy. Use the Word of God against him and, having submitted yourself to God, stand, and resist the devil, and take that place of victory in the Lord Jesus.

Looking unto Jesus.

Acknowledge that he is the giver of every good and perfect gift. He is the one who takes the Word, blesses it and breaks it and gives it to you. Ask him to help you receive it.

PRAYER

Father, open my eyes that I may see wonderful things out of your Word. Teach me to rest in you, and to hear your voice. Thank you, because I am in Christ and he is in me, I can resist all the power of the enemy and have your victory. Feed me with the meat of your Word, that I may be strong in the Lord, and in the power of his might. I desire a greater knowledge of yourself, and likeness to your beloved Son, Jesus. Therefore, open my understanding to the truths of meditating in your Word, and then help me in the practice of it in my daily walk with you.

Thank you that you will. Amen.

Let the words of my mouth and the meditation of my heart, be acceptable in thy sight, O Lord, my strength and my redeemer (Ps. 19:14).

My heart was hot within me, while I was musing the fire burned: then spake I with my tongue,
Lord, make me to know mine end, and the measure of my days, what it is; that I may know how frail I am (Ps. 39:3–4).

19 *Meditation . . .*

its practice (2)

Having seen the necessity of a restful but attentive attitude towards God, the dealing with our own thoughts, and resisting the work of the enemy, we now proceed to answer some very important questions.

Where should I meditate?

Because God knows our needs, and what he wishes us to learn, it is important to let him show us where to meditate. In doing this we are again acknowledging him in our ways, and it is important that we meditate according to his will and plan. Sometimes in the reading of the Word, a verse or verses come alive to us, and we have a desire to meditate on them, to receive all that God wishes to reveal, and that is good. However, because God is a God of order, and he has compiled the Bible in a very special way, it is most strongly recommended that the very best method of meditation is a systematic, verse by verse meditation, starting at chapter one and verse one of the book God shows you. This is said after years of personal experience, together with the experience and testimony of many others. It is also a safeguard, as consistent meditation keeps us within the context of the teaching, saving us from taking a verse out of its context to make it a pretext. Having meditated on the first verse, then move to the next, and so on, through to the end of the book.

So that you may start right, discover now where God wants you to meditate. We are going to put into practice the teaching of the previous chapter. You are going to ask God in which book of the Bible he wants you to meditate.

Ready? Tell the Lord you die to your own thoughts and choice of books, and you only want his will; then wait in silence for a few moments, and the first book that comes to your mind is God's answer for you. Pray your own prayer or follow this one.

Father, I come to you as your child, having chosen to meditate in your Word each day. I surrender my own choice, and die to my own desire, wanting only your will. Please show me now in which book you want me to meditate. Thank you, you will. Amen.

Wait quietly now before him. Now write down the book he has given. The Lord has shown me to meditate in ....
.... Date ....

When you have meditated through that book, then ask the Lord for the next one in the same way.

How long should I meditate?

The answer to this question is meditate until you have received from the Lord. One of the good things about meditation is that the word that has come to our hearts will continually return to our minds throughout the day, so that we can ponder it further. Initially, it is advised to set aside at least fifteen minutes. I know as you experience revelation from the Lord you probably will increase that time, but the main thing is to start, and then continue as your hunger and thirst for God increases. The Lord can give revelation of truth in a few minutes, or in a longer period. He knows our schedules, and he is always a rewarder of those who diligently seek him. All these things you will discover yourself as you become a meditator.

When is the best time to meditate?

One cannot be dogmatic or legalistic in answering this question. The best time is when you can sit down unhurriedly with the Lord. A mother with a young child or children will probably not find opportunity until mid-morning. People on shift work must adapt according to their work programme. However, because we have chosen to 'seek first the kingdom of God, and his righteousness', meditation is going to have priority in our lives with, of course, the other approaches to the Word. First thing in the morning is no doubt the best time when this is possible.

What should I do when I am not sure whether the thoughts are mine or his?

Sometimes this question may come to your mind. A simple way to deal with it is to ask the Lord that if it is not of himself (but out of your own mind), to fade it into the background; and if it is of him, to confirm it to you. He is such a wonderful teacher and friend, and he will respond to our requests and desires when he sees we really want to know him and to do his will. Also, when in doubt, certain questions can be asked to test whether it is of God, such as:

- Does it glorify God, and exalt the Lord Jesus?
- Is it edifying?
- Does it increase knowledge of him, and his ways?
- Is it in harmony with the rest of Scripture?
- Does it bring a response to God of prayer, praise,
- thanksgiving, worship, or confession?

Remember the words of the Lord Jesus: 'If any man will do do his will, he shall know of the doctrine, whether it be of God, or whether I speak of myself' (John 7:17).

What do I do if I am getting nothing from the verse?

If you ever experience a 'dry' period, and there seems to be no revelation coming to you from the Word, speak to the Lord about it. He loves honesty, and we can tell him exactly how we feel, and exactly what the situation is. There are obvious questions to ask ourselves such as:

- Have I obeyed what he has told me previously?
- Did I expect God to speak to me?
- Am I leaning to my own understanding?
- Am I relying on the Holy Spirit to lead me into all truth?
- Am I meditating so that I may know God?
- Have I waited on the Lord to receive from him, or have I been impatient?

If these questions do not reveal anything wrong in your life or attitude, rest in him; and if nothing is revealed in that particular verse, move on to the next one.

All true meditation will bring a response to God

In meditation God communes with us, and we with him. Earlier in the manual we shared George Muller's testimony, in which he said that meditation led him to confession, thanksgiving, intercession, or supplication, yet it turned always to prayer, that is, there was always a response to God. Part of meditation is praying the scriptures. That great saint of the seventeenth century, Mme. Jeanne Guyon, whose writings greatly influenced such saints as John Wesley and Jesse Penn Lewis, encouraged people to 'pray the scriptures'. She said that 'praying the scriptures' was not judged by how much was read, but by the way it was read. She said that reading quickly was like 'a bee skimming the surface of a flower, but praying the scriptures was like the bee penetrating into the depths of the flower to remove the deepest nectar'. One of the wonderful results of meditation is that God is going to receive much more from us, in prayer, praise, thanksgiving, worship and intercession. So let us again underline this truth, meditation always brings a response to God. Let us look at some scriptural evidences for this.

REFERENCE	VERSE	RESPONSE
Ps. 39:3–4	My heart was hot within me, while I was musing the fire burned;	Prayer then spake I with my tongue, Lord, make me to know mine end, and the measure of my days, what it is; that I may know how frail I am.
Ps. 63:5–6	When I remember thee upon my bed, and meditate on thee in the night watches.	Praise My soul shall be satisfied as with marrow and fatness, and my mouth shall praise thee with joyful lips.
Ps. 143:5–6	When I remember the days of old; I meditate on all thy works; I muse on the works of thy hands.	Expressed longing for God I stretch forth my hands unto thee, my soul thirsteth after thee as a thirsty land.
Ps. 119:48	I will meditate in thy statutes.	My hands also will I lift up unto thy commandments, which I have loved.
Ps. 77:12	I will meditate also of all thy work.	Speaking out and talk of all thy doings.
Ps. 49:3	The meditation of my heart shall be of understanding.	my mouth shall speak of wisdom.
Ps. 1:2	In his law doth he meditate day and night.	Delighting in the Word His delight is in the law of the Lord
Ps. 104:34	My meditation of him shall be sweet.	Joy I will be glad in the Lord.
I Tim. 4:15	Meditate upon these things.	Commital to truth Give thyself wholly to them.

The meanings of the word 'meditate' in the Hebrew and Greek indicate such a response. See Appendix A for details. In summary the word means: to mutter; to imagine; to speak; to study; to bow down; to make a solemn sound; to commune; to pray; to declare; to muse. These words confirm that meditation brings a response from mind, heart and will. Truth comes primarily to the intellect, and moves to the heart, which then in turn moves the will, resulting in total obedience to God.

Can I include study with meditation?

Sometimes while meditating on the scriptures there is a desire to know more about a particular word or subject which the verse or verses suggest. There is nothing wrong with gaining more knowledge through a concordance, commentary, or Bible dictionary. However, having gained that knowledge, bring it back to the verse and include it in your meditation.

How can I retain what I receive in meditation?

In meditation the Holy Spirit takes the Word of God and imparts it to our inner being. That word becomes part of us when it has been received. The Holy Spirit can also bring truth to our remembrance when required. Jesus taught the disciples this when he said:

But the Comforter, which is the Holy Ghost, whom the Father will send in my name, he shall teach you all things, and bring all things to your remembrance, whatsoever I have said unto you (John 14:26).

There are things we will not forget, but there are some things you may forget, such as other scriptures which have been brought to you while meditating. It is therefore good to have a Bible marking system, writing scripture references in the margin of your Bible, underlining or shading in certain important words, or connecting words or verses by drawn lines. Make your Bible your bank, so that the treasures God has given you are not lost. Some people prefer to keep a note book, or a daily diary of what the Lord has said and taught. Use what is best for you, and the means by which you will retain as much as possible.

Having dealt with some questions which could arise, let me now give you an illustration of meditation, and then you are ready to start your own, having received, I trust, the book in the Bible where you are going to begin.

And Isaac went out to meditate in the field at the eventide: and he lifted up his eyes, and saw, and behold, the camels were coming (Gen. 24:63).

This book of the law shall not depart out of thy mouth; but thou shalt meditate therein day and night (Josh. 1:8).

My son, attend to my words; incline thine ear unto my sayings.

Let them not depart from thine eyes; and keep them in the midst of thine heart.

For they are life unto those that find them, and health to all their flesh (Prov. 4:20–2).

20 *Meditation . . .*

demonstration

It may be helpful to give a brief demonstration of meditation, taking the opening verses of the book of Jonah. Firstly, there would be the quiet waiting on the Lord, as taught in a previous chapter, dealing with all distracting thoughts.

Prayer

Father, thank you for the joy of being in your presence, as I come to you in the name of the Lord Jesus. I thank you for making me your child, and for all your wonderful love to me, shown in so many different ways. I praise you for yourself, the giver of every good and perfect gift. I worship you for all that you are, and for all that the Lord Jesus is, in all your glorious majesty, holiness, purity and power. All that is within me blesses your holy name.

I have come to sit before you to hear you speak to me through your Word, and I thank you that you will. Would you please show me if there is anything in my life that is not pleasing to you ... any unconfessed sin ... (pause .... dealing with anything he shows).

Father, I die to my own thoughts and imaginations, and in the name of the Lord Jesus, I resist any work of the enemy, as I submit myself to you. (Satan and demon powers, I resist you in the name of the Lord Jesus, and any thoughts you would seek to plant in my mind. I am a blood-bought child of God, and have the victory through the blood of the Lamb and the word of my testimony.)

Dear Lord, fill me with your Spirit, and teach me from your Word, in Jesus' name. Amen.

The Word

(In commencing meditation in this chapter, I would first read through the whole chapter to have an understanding of the context; then go back and slowly read the first one or two verses unhurriedly, prayerfully, contemplatively, in faith and dependence on the Lord, to reveal truth to me.)

Now the word of the Lord came unto Jonah the son of Amittai, saying,
Arise, go to Nineveh, that great city, and cry against it; for their wickedness is come up before me.

Meditation and response

Now the word of the Lord came to Jonah – a clear and definite statement: God spoke.

Father, thank you that you speak, and as *Prayer* your word came clearly to Jonah, let your word come clearly to me.

Thank you, too, that when you speak it *Thanksgiving* means that you are with me, there could be no voice without you; so I praise you for your presence.

Thank you, too, Father, as you knew Jonah's name, you know mine too. I praise you for making me your son. Thank you for every word you have spoken to me, and for every word you are still going to speak. Thank you, you are God who speaks 'now'.

. . . the son of Amittai.

Father, you knew Jonah's father's name, *Intercession* too. I thank you for my father, now in your presence, and for his godly life which was such an example, and for his loving affection and care. Please help me to be a good father and a blessing to my family. God bless them today, and keep them in your name. Let your good hand be on Stuart and Celia and their two lovely children, Charis and Ewan; on dear Patricia and Sandra, and dear John and Joy. Reveal to me any specific needs they may have as I wait upon you . . .

(If you were meditating on these verses, you could pray for your father if he is alive, bringing any needs you know he has, or that the Lord shows you he has).

Here, as a matter of interest, I looked up the meaning of the names Jonah and Amittai in my Young's concordance, and found that Jonah means 'a dove', and Amittai means 'truth' . . . so I ponder this information, and include it in my meditation. The dove is one of the emblems of the Holy Spirit . . . I look up Matthew 3:16–17. (While meditating, other scriptures come to your mind; look them up, and read them, thus your meditation is extended).

And Jesus, when he was baptized, went up straightway out of the water: and, lo, the heavens were opened unto him, and he saw the Spirit of God descending like a dove, and lighting upon him:
And lo a voice from heaven, saying, This is my beloved Son, in whom I am well pleased.

Thank you Lord Jesus, you who are *truth*, for dying, and rising from the dead, and as-cending to heaven, and sending the Holy Spirit, the heavenly dove, to teach me, and lead me into all truth as you promised he would. Bring the Word to me and through me to others by the power of the Holy Spirit.

Thanksgiving

Prayer

Meditation and response

Arise, go to Nineveh, that great city, and cry against it; for their wickedness is come up before me.

It is good to know that God is concerned about cities. Jesus wept over Jerusalem, and was concerned about Capernaum. It is good to know that God is concerned over my city, San Jose, California, and all other cities. It is interesting how simple God's instructions were to Jonah . . . nothing obscure or complicated . . . and that's right. Although there are some deep truths and doctrines, his instructions are always clear to me. That's a comfort. 'Arise . . . go to Nineveh . . . cry against it' – so clear and specific. Lord, apply this verse to me . . . thank you, I sense you want me to pray for my city.

Father, I call on your name and pray for San Jose . . . lead me by your Spirit. I pray for all your people in the city, and for every church that honours you. I pray for my own home church, Calvary Community Church, for my beloved Pastor Gerald Fry and his dear wife, Peggy, and all my brothers and sisters, for whom I thank you. Let your mighty hand be upon us continually, and make us an instrument of blessing to the city, the state and the nation, and other parts of the world. Let there there be an ever increasing unity among all thy people, so that it will be known that we are thy disciples because we have love one to another. Please give me the privilege of being one of your instruments for this purpose. I present to you the mayor, and councilmen, and ask you Lord, to give them a heart desire for righteousness in our city. As you looked on Nineveh, and saw their wickedness, yet desired to send your messenger – so you see all the wickedness of our city. Have mercy upon us, O God, and let salvation visit this city. Show us your ways and your plans. We die to our own good ideas.

Intercession

148

Save souls in the city. Prosper every
means you have raised up to make the
good news of the gospel known, in Jesus'
name.

*But Jonah rose up to flee unto Tarshish from the presence
of the Lord, and went down to Joppa . . .*

That little three letter word spoils the story: 'but' . . . it
has spoiled other stories too. It spoiled the great story of
Solomon: 'But King Solomon loved many strange wives' —
and God had told him not to multiply to himself wives, so
disobedience marred a good life. I remember another king,
Uzziah, who started well and finished badly because of a
'but'.

Father, I do not want to have any 'buts' of
disobedience in my life. Are there any
Lord? ....
I do not want to run away from your
plan and purposes for my life.
I trust you to make your will and instructions so clear to me that I cannot
mistake them; and Lord, I want to obey.
Please help me, and I trust you to do
this. Amen.

And so meditation would be continued. Although most of
the thoughts from Jonah were received in meditation some
time ago, the prayers I have shared were spontaneous.

Please note that meditation is a very personal thing. It
is God speaking to *me*. Not a sermon for someone else
initially, but truth that must be applied to the heart. Note,
too, the variety of responses that can come from a few
minutes of meditation: thanksgiving, praise, prayer, and
intercession. Having meditated on these verses, not only
will they return constantly to the mind, but the verses are
often retained in the memory, so that a bank of scriptures
is stored up in the vault of memorisation.

21 *Meditation . . .*

your beginning

This is the day you can start as a meditator, putting into practise the things you have been learning.

Wait on the Lord

Be still . . . then speak to the Lord in thanksgiving (for what he has done for you); in praise (for who he is); in worship (the outpouring of your love); in confession of your trust in him to speak to you, as you surrender your own thoughts; to have the mind of Christ.

Open your Bible now, at chapter one. If you have not already read the first chapter, do that now.

Date . . . . . . Today I started meditating in the book of . . . . .

As an aid to starting, write out the first two or three verses:

Meditation and responses:

Summary

What did I learn of God today? ....
....

What did I learn about myself? ....
....

What did I praise him for? ....
....

What and who did I pray for or intercede for? ....
....

Finish your meditation with worship

Choose to recall your meditation throughout the day and night, and you will find the Lord will keep giving you more, as well as establishing what you have received.

22 Meditation . . .

your continuance

This is your second day . . . well done. Remember what the Lord said to you yesterday? It has remained, hasn't it? Thank the Lord.

Wait on the Lord.

Date . . . . . Book . . . . . . Chapter 1, verse(s) . . . . .

Write out the verses you are meditating on today.

Meditation and responses:

Summary of my meditation:

As you finish by thanking the Lord, tell him you are available to share with others what he has shared with you as he opens the way and directs. People like 'fresh bread'.

23 *Meditation . . .*

your progress

This is your third day, and already you are experiencing the blessing of meditation. We will not go beyond this in the manual: (that is, recording your meditation in this book). Keep this book as your own personal record and diary of launching out into a new, wonderful venture of knowing God more.

Wait on the Lord.

Date . . . . . .   Book . . . . . .   Chapter 1, verse(s) . . . . .

Write out the verses. (You need not always do this, but it is a help in the learning stage of meditation.)

Meditation and response:

Summary of my meditation:

As you finish today, would you ask the Lord to show you someone that you could teach to meditate. If this manual has helped you, encourage them to get one, or buy one for them.

And now, brethren, I commend you to God, and to the Word of his grace, which is able to build you up, and to give you an inheritance among all them which are sanctified (Acts 20:32).

Sanctify them through thy truth: the Word is truth (John 17:17).

If ye continue in my Word, then are ye my disciples indeed; and ye shall know the truth, and the truth shall make you free (John 8:31–2).

Being born again, not of corruptible seed, but of incorruptible, by the Word of God, which liveth and abideth for ever.

For all flesh is as grass, and all the glory of man as the flower of grass. The grass withereth, and the flower thereof falleth away:

But the Word of the Lord endureth for ever. And this is the Word which by the gospel is preached unto you (1 Pet. 1:23–5).

24 *Meditation . . .*

its product

The Word of God is a treasure which produces great riches in and from the lives of those who meditate in it. In the King James version of the Bible, one can read the letter the translators wrote to the king, when they submitted the new version to him. It includes this good statement:

> But among all our joys, there was no one that more filled our hearts, than the blessed continuance of the preaching of God's sacred Word among us; which is that inestimable treasure, which excelleth all the riches of the earth; because the fruit thereof extendeth itself, not only to the time spent in this transitory world, but directeth and disposeth men unto that eternal happiness which is above in heaven.

How true, as we receive the Word it does 'extend itself'. Because it is life, it produces life; and that life is manifested in the one who has chosen to be a 'doer of the Word'. When that happens we will be the people that Paul described as:

Ye are our epistle written in our hearts, known and read of all men (2 Cor. 3:2).

We saw from Psalm 1 that meditation produces happiness, fruitfulness, and prosperity. As a further encouragement to continue, let us discover from David in Psalm 119 how meditation affected his life in varying circumstances, and therefore how it will affect ours.

Meditation causes us to respect God's ways

I will meditate in thy precepts, and have respect unto thy ways (v. 15).

As David pondered, and considered the commands and directions of God in meditation it caused him to give them his full respect. The result was joyous obedience, because in the next verse he declares:

I will delight myself in thy statutes: I will not forget thy word (v. 16).

Meditation strengthens us to resist temptation

David received so much opposition in his life from enemies from without and enemies from within. He was the subject of criticism and judgment, yet he testifies that meditation prevented him from wrong reactions. He says:

Princes also did sit and speak against me: but thy servant did meditate in thy statutes (v. 23).

As his Word is received within our hearts, the more our behaviour will resemble his, 'who, when he was reviled, reviled not again'. He did not retaliate, but went to the cross and 'bare our sins in his own body on the tree' (1 Pet. 2:23–4). The word, 'statute' is an interesting word. It means 'within a decreed limit'. The decreed limit for the child of God is the will of God; and the knowledge of his Word, and obedience to it, will keep us within that perfect will.

There is an incident in the life of David which illustrates this truth. When Absalom, David's son, rose up in rebellion against him, David fled from Jerusalem. As he was going a man called Shimei followed him, cursing him, 'Come out, come out thou bloody man, and thou man of Belial,' and threw stones at David and the men that were with him. One of David's men, Abishai, wanted to go and remove Shimei's head from his shoulders, but David wouldn't allow him. Later when Solomon succeeded his father, he sent for Shimei, knowing how he had treated his father. He told Shimei to live in Jerusalem, but set definite boundaries for him, telling him that if he crossed over these boundaries his life would be forfeit. In other words, he set a statute – a decreed limit. Shimei was perfectly free and safe as long as he obeyed the king. Three years later, two of Shimei's servants left him and ran away outside the city and Shimei went after them and brought them back home. When Solomon heard this he sent for Shimei and said, 'Why then hast thou not kept the oath of the Lord, and the commandment that I have charged thee with?' Because he had deliberately disobeyed the word of the king, he was slain.

Our place of absolute safety, protection and joy is within the will of God, which we discover and learn from his Word. While princes spoke against David he meditated in God's decreed limits, accepting them, and thus enabling him to overcome temptation and obey God.

Meditation produces an increased love for the Word

The more we taste and eat of the good Word of God, the larger become our appetites and love for it. When you eat the best, it causes you to lose taste for anything that is inferior.

> **Butter and honey shall he eat, that he may know to refuse the evil, and choose the good** (Isa. 7:15).

David's meditation in the Word, and obedience to it, obviously produced an ever increasing love for all that God had said:

> **I will delight myself in thy commandments, which I have loved.**
> **My hands also will I lift up unto thy commandments, which I have loved; and I will meditate in thy statutes** (Ps. 119:47–8).

> **O how love I thy law! it is my meditation all the day** (v. 97).

This will be your experience too, as you continue.

Meditation gives understanding as well as knowledge

David prayed in verse 34, 'Give me understanding, and I shall keep thy law; yea, I shall observe it with my whole heart.' With this desire and determination to obey God, it is not surprising to read later in verses 99–100:

> **I have more understanding than all my teachers: for thy testimonies are my meditation.**
> **I understand more than the ancients, because I keep thy precepts.**

Notice he did not say he had more knowledge than his teachers, but more understanding. Knowledge without understanding does not profit; and one of the products of meditation is the understanding of the Word. Some Christians have not had much education, but God has taught them and given them tremendous insights of truth, and the ways of God.

Some years ago I was ministering in a church in England, and was being hosted by a delightful elderly Christian and his wife. We had been speaking together about understanding and knowledge, and he told me a story out of his own experience which illustrated this. When he was a young man he had gone to one of their denominational conferences. Sitting on the platform was a man in a rough suit, with his head leaning to one side, and his mouth partially open. He asked a friend, 'Who is that?' He was told that he was the speaker; a farm labourer who had left school at the age of twelve. So he said he sat back, waiting for the worst! After the hymn singing and prayer, this big man stood up, came forward to the rostrum, stretched his arms out and quoted the verse of a hymn:

> O Christ what burdens bowed thy head,
> My sin was laid on thee,
> Thou sufferedst in the sinners stead,
> Took all the guilt for me.

He said suddenly the place was filled with the presence of the Lord. Then he opened the Bible and give us honey out of the rock. So impressed and blessed was my friend, that he went to the preacher afterwards and asked him where he got such great truths. He told him that he rose early every morning, lit a candle, got dressed, and read one or two verses over and over again. Then he would put his coat on, and would walk up and down the country lane, allowing the Holy Spirit to take the truth he had read from his head to his heart. That is where I get it all, he said. Although uneducated, God had given him understanding as he meditated on the Word. You do not need a high I.Q. to meditate, just an open heart to be taught of God. David said in verse 102, 'thou hast taught me'. On the other hand it is also wonderful to see a brilliant intellect dedicated to the glory of God; but both are dependent on the Holy Spirit to give divine illumination and understanding.

Meditation is better than sleeping pills

David had some sleepless nights, but he even took advantage of this to meditate.

I prevented the dawning of the morning, and cried: I hoped in thy word.
Mine eyes prevent the night watches, that I might meditate in thy word (Ps. 119:147–8).

It is the testimony of many meditators that when they have been wakeful in the night, they have continued to meditate on the verses they were considering during the day, and during such meditation they have fallen asleep. That is better than counting sheep. Remember the blessing in Psalm 1 is to the person who meditates 'day and night'.

See Appendix B for a summary of the consequences of meditation in Psalm 119.

APPLICATION

It is so important that you not only start to meditate but that you continue. The temptation will come one day to miss your meditation, and perhaps do twice as much tomorrow! Sometimes this happens, but tomorrow becomes very busy too. When you overcome the first temptation, and determine to get to know God each day through his Word, you will find it easier to overcome the same temptation when it comes the next time. Think of all the blessings, advantages and products of meditation, and continue.

PRAYER

Father, I want to continue to thank you for the treasure house of the Word of God, containing truth and revelation that no wealth on earth could buy. I want to be a diligent seeker of truth, not only receiving knowledge, but also understanding. Thank you that your Word will cause me to respect your ways and walk in them; strengthen me to resist temptation; help me not to react in the flesh. I praise you that my love for you and the Word will also increase, and like David, I will delight myself in your commandments; and incline my heart to your testimonies. When I awake in the night, then speak to me through your Word, so that my knowledge of you will be expanded, for your glory. Amen.

Till I come, give attendance to reading, to exhortation, to doctrine. . .

Meditate upon these things; give thyself wholly to them; that thy profiting may appear to all.

Take heed to thyself, and unto the doctrine; continue in them: for in doing this thou shalt both save thyself, and them that hear thee (1 Tim. 4:13,15–16).

And now, brethren, I commend you to God, and to the word of his grace, which is able to build you up, and to give you an inheritance among all them which are sanctified (Acts 20:32).

25 *Meditation . . .*

its subjects

There are several themes upon which we can meditate, as we discover in the life of David. These are:

The Word of God

Most of the latter part of this manual has been devoted to meditation in the Word, so we will not add anything to what has gone before.

On God, and his Son, the Lord Jesus

There are many times when we can meditate on God, and on the Lord Jesus, even without an open Bible. We can do this in the silence of waiting on God, contemplating his greatness; pondering the great faithfulness of God, remembering personal experiences of such faithfulness. Pondering on the wonders of himself, his glory, goodness, holiness, justice, longsuffering, love, mercy, power, wisdom, grace, judgments, knowledge. What will be the result? We will be lost in 'wonder, love and praise'. Worship will arise to our God for all that he is. We can meditate on his names which portray the beauty of his character and the loveliness of his person.

David said:

My meditation of *him* shall be sweet: I will be glad in the Lord (Ps. 104:34).

My soul shall be satisfied as with marrow and fatness; and my mouth shall praise thee with joyful lips;

> When I remember *thee* upon my bed, and meditate on
> *thee* in the night watches (Ps. 63:5–6).

The work of God

> I will remember the *works of the Lord*: surely I will
> remember thy *wonders* of old.
> I will meditate also of all thy *work*, and talk of thy doings
> (Ps. 77:11–12).

Remembering all that God has done in the past is not only
an incentive to praise, but a stimulus to faith. Many times
in scriptures the writers deliberately bring to remembrance
the works of God. 'Remember his marvellous works that he
hath done; his wonders, and the judgments of his mouth,'
cries David in Psalm 105:5. Many of the psalms are taken
up with the mighty works of God in the past; which encourages us to trust him for the present and for the future.
In Deuteronomy 32, Moses recounted many of God's works
before the children of Israel just prior to his death and their
entry into the promised land. Joshua did the same before
his death, and having encouraged them by such remembr-
ances exhorted them to serve the Lord in sincerity and
truth.

You, too, can remember the works of the Lord, either in
the Word, in history, in your nation, or in your personal
life; and such meditation will bring praise to God, and
encouragement to you to trust him.

The works of God's hands

Not only did the psalmist meditate on the works of God, but
also on the works of his hands:

> I remember the days of old; I meditate on all thy works; I
> muse on the *work of thy hands*.
> I stretch forth my hands unto thee: my soul thirsteth after
> thee, as a thirsty land (Ps. 143:5–6).

God spoke to many of his servants through his creation
or creatures. Before God gave Abraham the promise of the

multiplication of his seed, he told him to contemplate the works of his hands, the stars:

And he brought him forth abroad, and said, Look now toward heaven, and tell the *stars*, if thou be able to number them: and he said unto him, So shall thy seed be (Gen. 15:5).

If we have eyes to see, there is so much which declares his greatness and causes us to worship and praise him.

The *heavens* declare the glory of God; and the firmament showeth his handywork.
Day unto day uttereth speech, and night unto night sheweth knowledge.
There is no speech nor language, where their voice is not heard (Ps. 19:1–3).

We are even asked to consider one of the very smallest works of his hands, the ant!

Go to the ant, thou sluggard; consider her ways, and be wise:
Which having no guide, overseer, or ruler,
Provideth her meat in the summer, and gathereth her food in the harvest (Prov. 6:6–8).

Yes, God speaks in so many ways and teaches so many lessons – from a corn of wheat; seed that falls into the ground; the trees; a rock; the grass; the lily of the field; the thunder and lightning; rain; dew; a spring of water; a watered garden; a mustard seed.

The 'God who at sundry times and in divers manners spake in time past', still speaks today in such a variety of ways. Meditation quickens our senses to be perceptive to what he is saying, either in the Word, while meditating on himself, or his work, or the works of his hands. May our attitude always be, 'Speak Lord, for thy servant heareth' – and expect an answer.

26 *The final bugle*

The call to meditate is not a polite evangelical request to adopt a useful technique that will brighten up the quiet time. Rather it is a command to be disciplined; to think clearly; to be prepared; to be watchful; and above all, to know God and his Son, Jesus Christ. We should consider it as a clear instruction from God which deserves our attention and obedience:

You shall meditate therein day and night (Josh. 1:8).

Set your hearts unto all the words which I testify among you this day (Deut. 32:46).

Ponder the path of thy feet (Prov. 4:26).

Consider your ways (Hagg. 1:7).

Let these sayings sink down into your ears (Luke 9:44).

Whatsoever things are true . . . think on these things (Phil. 4:8).

We are living in days of gross darkness. The effects of evil are going to become more evident in our society. The Church will be purified; and there will be a separation of true from false, real from counterfeit. Much of Paul's writing in the epistles is directed by an awareness of the perilous circumstances of those to whom he wrote. As year succeeds year, it seems that our circumstances as believers, in the society in which we now live, places us in the same context as Paul's readers. As I write, there has been an earthquake, and the study in which I sit has been severely shaken – a frightening sensation. How much more frightening when God shakes the foundations, and the weakness of the superstructures that we have dared to impose on the kingdom of God collapse like balsa wood.

The Church has been characterised too often as an institution that is constantly sitting down at meetings, at conferences, at cross-denominational this, and cross that discussions ... the irony being, that the impact and demands of the cross of Christ have not surfaced through the agenda.

The call to meditate is a call to heed the words of God, because only his words minister life; release light; illuminate our thinking on the greatest matters that we can know – the mighty character of God, and his purposes for our lives, the Church, the world and for eternity.

There is a great need in our day to be sharpened, and to be more urgent in the way we approach the things of God. Assurance has so often led to a kind of self-contented smugness that has strangled our spiritual life. In many areas some 'movements' have led to the cultivation of their own gardens, which bloom unmindful of the spiritual defoliation that has been wrecked by the havoc of the war of darkness against the souls of men. To meditate is to be continually exposed to the work of the Holy Spirit, who through the Word of God will lead us from self examination to an examination of the world in which we live. As we observe with the eyes of God, we will be mobilised to give our lives even as God was moved to give his only begotten Son. We will not overcome with church models, or our corporate personality. The abiding Word of God is the means of overcoming the wicked one.

We must repent of our sloth in our dealings with God's Word. The 'fruit salad' of religious ideas is served with doctrinal 'casseroles', and we are content with a state of affairs in the Church of the living God which would not be tolerated in a school or business. The command to meditate, ringing with the urgency of the heart of God, is a command to think his thoughts, and to learn of him. How will you fare in the battle which wages for the minds of men, without the mind of God? We must mentally develop! Meditation will leave you in no doubt that the Christian mind has a wholly supernatural orientation, and will convince you that it is only as the Word of God abides in you, that you will survive the violent collision between the mind of Christ and earthly culture. It is the life of Christ in us that will remain unshaken.

We must determine to commit ourselves to new levels of mental concentration and application in the work of God, and in the walk of faith. The Bible is filled with encouraging yet urgent injunctions to be mentally alert, and spiritually watchful; and all such words deserve thoughtful reflection and earnest contemplation and meditation. This will keep us free from being 'puffed up' by knowledge which is void of spiritual revelation, but will number us among those who, with humble and contrite hearts, continually yearn to know God, so that the glorying will be as Jeremiah recorded:

> ... let him that glorieth, glory in this, that he understandeth and knoweth me, that I am the Lord which exercise lovingkindness, judgment, and righteousness, in the earth: for in these things I delight, saith the Lord (Jer. 9:24).

Appendix A

Summary of scriptures using the word 'meditation'

Hagah = to meditate; to mutter

This book of the law shall not depart out of thy mouth; but thou shalt meditate therein day and night, that thou mayest observe to do according to all that is written therein: for then thou shalt make thy way prosperous, and then thou shalt have good success.	Joshua 1:8

But his delight is in the law of the Lord; and in his law doth he meditate day and night.

Psalm 1:2

When I remember thee upon my bed, and meditate on thee in the night watches.

Psalm 63:6

I will meditate also of all thy work, and talk of thy doings.

Psalm 77:12

I remember the days of old; I meditate on all thy works: I muse on the work of thy hands.

Psalm 143:5

Thine heart shall meditate terror. Where is the scribe? where is the receiver? where is he that counted the towers?

Isaiah 33:18

Other meanings of the word 'hagah'

1. *To imagine*
Why do the heathen rage, and the people imagine a vain thing?

Psalm 2:1

They also that seek after my life lay snares for me: and they that seek my hurt speak mischievous things, and *imagine* deceits all the day long.

Psalm 38:12

2. *To mourn*
Therefore shall Moab howl for Moab, every one shall howl: for the foundations of Kir-hareseth shall ye *mourn*; surely they are stricken.

Isaiah 16:7

Like a crane or a swallow, so did I chatter: I did *mourn* as a dove: mine eyes fail with looking upward: O Lord, I am oppressed; undertake for me.

Isaiah 38:14

3. *Mutter*
For your hands are defiled with blood, and your fingers with iniquity; your lips have spoken lies, your tongue hath *muttered* perverseness.

Isaiah 59:3

4. *Roar*
For thus hath the Lord spoken unto me, like as a lion and the young lion *roaring* on his prey, when a multitude of shepherds is called forth against him, he will not be afraid of their voice, nor abase himself for the noise of them: so shall the Lord of hosts come down to fight for Mount Zion, and for the hill thereof.

Isaiah 31:4

5. *Speak*
And my tongue shall *speak* of thy righteousness and of thy praise all the day long.

Psalm 35:28

The mouth of the righteous *speaketh* wisdom, and his tongue talketh of judgment.

Psalm 37:30

For my mouth shall *speak* truth; and wickedness is an abomination to my lips.

Proverbs 8:7

6. *Study*

The heart of the righteous *studieth* to answer: but the mouth of the wicked poureth out evil things.

Proverbs 15:28

7. *Talk*

My tongue also shall *talk* of thy righteousness all the day long: for they are confounded, for they are brought unto shame, that seek my hurt.

Psalm 71:24

8. *Utter*

My lips shall not speak wickedness, nor my tongue *utter* deceit.

Job 27:4

Siach = to bow down, to muse, to meditate

And Isaac went out to meditate in the field at the eventide: and he lifted up his eyes and saw, and behold, the camels were coming.

Genesis 24:63

I will meditate in thy precepts, and have respect unto thy ways.

Psalm 119:15

Princes also did sit and speak against me: but thy servant did meditate in thy statutes.

Psalm 119:23

My hands also will I lift up unto thy commandments, which I have loved; and I will meditate in thy statutes.

Psalm 119:48

Let the proud be ashamed; for they dealt perversely with me without a cause: but I will meditate in thy precepts.

Psalm 119:78

Mine eyes prevent the night watches, that I might meditate in thy word.

Psalm 119:148

My meditation of him shall be sweet: I will be glad in the Lord.

Psalm 104:34

180

Other meanings of the word 'siach'

1. *Commune*
I call to remembrance my song in the night: I
commune with mine own heart: and my spirit
made diligent search.

Psalm 77:6

2. *Complain*
Therefore I will not refrain my mouth; I will
speak in the anguish of my spirit; I will *com-
plain* in the bitterness of my soul.

Job 7:11

I remembered God and was troubled: I *com-
plained*, and my spirit was overwhelmed.

Psalm 77:3

3. *Pray*
Evening and morning, and at noon, will I *pray*,
and cry aloud: and he shall hear my voice.

Psalm 55:17

4. *Speak, converse*
Speak, ye that ride on white asses, ye that sit
in judgment, and walk by the way.

Judges 5:10

I will *speak* of the glorious honour of thy majesty, and of thy wondrous works.

Psalm 145:5

5. *Talk*
Sing unto him, sing psalms unto him, *talk* ye
of all his wondrous works.

1 Chronicles 16:9

Make me to understand the way of thy precepts: so shall I *talk* of thy wondrous works.

Psalm 119:27

When thou goest, it shall lead thee; when thou
sleepest, it shall keep thee; and when thou
awakest, it shall *talk* with thee.

Proverbs 6:22

Promeletao = to take care beforehand

Settle it therefore in your hearts, not to *med-*   Luke 21:14
itate before what ye shall answer.

Meletao = to be careful; to take care

Meditate upon these things; give thyself whol-   1 Timothy 4:15
ly to them; that thy profiting may appear to
all.
(also used as premeditate in Mark 13:11)

Hagig = earnest meditation; musing

Give ear to my words, O Lord, consider my   Psalm 5:1
meditation.

My heart was hot within me, while I was *mus-*   Psalm 39:3
ing the fire burned: then spake I with my
tongue.

Higgayon = meditation; device; solemn sound

Let the words of my mouth, and the *meditation*   Psalm 19:14
of my heart, be acceptable in thy sight, O Lord,
my strength, and my Redeemer.

The lips of those that rose up against me, and Lamentations 3:62
their *device* against me all the day.

It is good to give thanks unto the Lord, and to   Psalm 92:1–3
sing praises unto thy name, O most high:
   To show forth thy lovingkindness in the
morning, and thy faithfulness every night,
   Upon an instrument of ten strings, and upon
the psaltery; upon the harp with a *solemn
sound.*

The Lord is known by the judgment which he   Psalm 9:16
executeth: the wicked is snared in the work of
his own hands. Higgaion, Selah.

Appendix B

Psalm 119: consequences of meditation in the law of the Lord

sincerity, safeguard against defilement (1)
saved from doing iniquity (3)
not ashamed (6)
praise (7)
cleansing of one's way (9)
avoidance of sin (11)
release in communication about God (13)
respect for God's ways (15)
stops forgetfulness (16)
increases longing for God (20)
shelters from slander (23)
counsel from the Word (24)
freedom to talk of God's wondrous works (27)
relief from heaviness (28)
restraint from lying (29)
enlargement of heart (32)
saved from covetousness (36)
turns away from vanity (37)
protection from reproach of others (39)
quickens in righteousness (40)
understanding of mercies and salvation of God (41)
liberty (45)
freedom to witness (46)
reason to hope (49)
comfort in affliction (50)
saves from wrong influence (51)
gives an understanding of the horror of sin (53)
inspires songs (54)
basis for intercession (58)
one of the grounds for fellowship (63)

increased understanding of God's goodness (68)
gives one a right view of possessions (72)
gives an understanding of God's creative purposes (73)
confirms truth about God's faithfulness amidst adversity (86)
proves the fixity and everlasting nature of God's Word (89)
expands our understanding (96)
increased love for the Word of God (97)
more understanding than teachers (99)
determination to avoid evil (101)
understanding of and hate for evil ways (104)
enlightenment and guidance (105)
content for worship (111)
hate for vain thoughts (113)
avoidance of wrong company (115)
fear of God (120)
deliverance from oppression of man (134)
compassion for lost (136)
understanding of God's righteousness (137)
understanding of the character of the Word of God (138–44)
source of salvation (155)
source of great riches (162)
great peace (165)
no stumbling-blocks (165)
ability to testify (172)

Summary of the meanings of the word 'meditation'

To mutter	To muse
To imagine	To commune
To mourn	To complain
To roar	To pray
To speak	To speak
To study	To be careful
To talk	To devise
To utter	To make a solemn sound
To bow down	